FRESH DESIGNS
KIDS

FEATURING DESIGNS BY

Elizabeth Green Musselman
Ellen Boucher
Hannah Cuviello
Hannah Ingalls
Kourtney Robinson
Peggy Bumgardner
Rachel Henry
Sharon Fuller
Stéphanie Voyer
Terri Kruse

AND PHOTOGRAPHY BY

Caro Sheridan

COOPERATIVE PRESS
Cleveland, OH
cooperativepress.com

FRESH DESIGNS: KIDS

ISBN 13: 978-1-937513-28-3
First Edition
Published by Cooperative Press
http://www.cooperativepress.com

Patterns © 2013, their designers, as credited
Photos © 2013, Caro Sheridan, Elizabeth Green Musselman

Models: Asa O., Asa W., Bailey Kate R., Declan R., Olivia C.

Every effort has been made to ensure that all the information in this book is accurate at the time of publication; however, Cooperative Press neither endorses nor guarantees the content of external links referenced in this book.

If you have questions or comments about this book, or need information about licensing, custom editions, special sales, or academic/corporate purchases, please contact Cooperative Press: info@cooperativepress.com or 13000 Athens Ave C288, Lakewood, OH 44107 USA

No part of this book may be reproduced in any form, except brief excerpts for the purpose of review, without prior written permission of the publisher. Thank you for respecting our copyright.

FOR COOPERATIVE PRESS

Senior Editor: Shannon Okey
Art Director and Editor: Elizabeth Green Musselman
Developmental Editor: Abra Forman
Technical Editor: Alexandra Virgiel
Cover Designer: Tamas Jakab
Production Manager: MJ Kim

TABLE OF CONTENTS

ELIZABETH GREEN MUSSELMAN	Treads Hoodie	(page 5)
ELLEN BOUCHER	Weinig Wortel	(page 9)
HANNAH CUVIELLO	Elsiebelle Sundress	(page 13)
HANNAH INGALLS	Superkid Sweater	(page 19)
KOURTNEY ROBINSON	Petal Bonnet	(page 25)
PEGGY BUMGARDNER	Jack & Clara Wintry Ensemble	(page 29)
RACHEL HENRY	Susan's Sunsuit	(page 37)
SHARON FULLER	Birdboots	(page 41)
STÉPHANIE VOYER	Funkyds Vest	(page 45)
TERRI KRUSE	Fireman's Cardi	(page 51)

ACKNOWLEDGMENTS	(page 55)
ABBREVIATIONS	(page 56)
ABOUT COOPERATIVE PRESS AND THE FRESH DESIGNS SERIES	(page 57)

TREADS HOODIE
BY ELIZABETH GREEN MUSSELMAN

DIFFICULTY

INTERMEDIATE

Variegated yarns can be tricky to work with, but this hoodie maximizes the possibilities in all that color. Knit in one piece, this sweater comes pre-kid-approved as "cool" but also (because of the lighter weight yarn) "not too hot."

SIZES
Approx age 4 [6, 8, 10, 12, 14] years (shown in size 8)

FINISHED MEASUREMENTS
Chest 26.25 [27.75, 30.5, 32, 33.5, 35]"/65.5 [69, 76.5, 80, 83.5, 87.5]cm

MATERIALS
[MC] Yarn Love Amy March [100% superwash merino wool; 270 yd/247m per 113g skein]; color: Earl Grey; 3 [4, 4, 5, 5, 6] skeins

[CC] Yarn Love Amy March [100% superwash merino wool; 270 yd/247m per 113g skein]; color: Tulips; 1 [1, 1, 1, 2, 2] skein(s)

Set of US #5/3.75mm double-point needles
Set of US #7/4.5mm double-point needles
24-inch US #5/3.75mm circular needle
24-inch US #7/4.5mm circular needle

Stitch markers
Yarn needle

GAUGE
22 sts/31 rows = 4"/10cm in stockinette on larger needles
22 sts/26 rows = 4"/10cm in charted Treads pattern on larger needles

PATTERN NOTES
This sweater is worked in the round from the bottom up. Body and sleeves are worked separately to the underarm, then joined and worked in one piece to the neck.

Garment is designed to be worn with 3–4"/8–10cm of positive ease.

PATTERN
Sleeves
With MC and smaller dpns, CO 32 [36, 40, 40, 44, 48] sts. Pm and join to work in the round.
Work Rnds 1–10 of Rib chart twice. Change to larger needles and stockinette.
Inc Rnd: K1, m1, knit to last st, m1, k1.
Rep Inc Rnd on every 6th rnd 10 [1, 2, 2, 2, 0] more times, then every 8th rnd 0 [9, 8, 9, 10, 12] times. 54 [58, 62, 64, 70, 74] sts.
Work even until sleeve measures 12 [13, 14, 15.5, 16, 17]"/30.5 [33, 35.5, 39.5, 40.5, 43]cm from CO.
Next rnd: Knit to last 4 [4, 5, 5, 6, 6] sts, loosely BO 8 [8, 10, 10, 12, 12] sts removing marker; knit to end. 46 [50, 52, 54, 58, 62] sts rem.
Cut yarn. Place sts on holder and set aside.

Body
With MC and smaller circular needle, CO 144 [152, 168, 176, 184, 192] sts. Pm and join to work in the round. Work Rnds 1–10 of Rib chart twice. Change to larger needle. Work Treads chart until body measures 9 [10.5, 12, 14.5, 16, 17]"/23 [26.5, 30.5, 37, 40.5, 43]cm. Cut CC.
With MC, knit 1 rnd.
Next rnd: P72 [76, 84, 88, 92, 96], pm for side, purl to last 4 [4, 5, 5, 6, 6] sts.
Next rnd: Loosely BO 8 [8, 10, 10, 12, 12] sts removing beg-of-rnd marker, knit to 4 [4, 5, 5, 6, 6] sts before side marker, loosely BO 8 [8, 10, 10, 12, 12] sts removing marker, knit to end. 64 [68, 74, 78, 80, 84] sts rem for front and for back. Do not cut yarn.

Yoke

Join body and sleeves: Using circular needle holding body sts and MC attached to body, k46 [50, 52, 54, 58, 62] sts of one sleeve, pm for beg of rnd, knit across 64 [68, 74, 78, 80, 84] front sts, pm, k46 [50, 52, 54, 58, 62] sts of second sleeve, pm, knit across 64 [68, 74, 78, 80, 84] back sts, pm, knit to end of rnd. 220 (236, 252, 264, 276, 292) sts.

Raglan Dec Rnd: *Ssk, knit to 2 sts before marker, k2tog, sl m; rep from * 3 more times. 8 sts dec'd.

Rep Raglan Dec Rnd on every 2nd rnd 8 [12, 14, 14, 16, 17] more times. 148 [132, 132, 144, 140, 148] sts rem: 46 [42, 44, 48, 46, 48] each for front and back, and 28 [24, 22, 24, 24, 26] for each sleeve. Work 1 rnd even.

Next rnd: Ssk, k16 [14, 15, 17, 16, 17], p10, k16 [14, 15, 17, 16, 17], k2tog, sl m, *ssk, knit to 2 sts before marker, k2tog, sl m; rep from * twice more. 140 [124, 124, 136, 132, 140] sts rem. Work 1 rnd even.

Next rnd: Ssk, k15 [13, 14, 16, 15, 16], p10, k15 [13, 14, 16, 15, 16], k2tog, sl m, *ssk, knit to 2 sts before marker, k2tog, sl m; rep from * twice more. 132 [116, 116, 128, 124, 132] sts rem.

Divide for neck:
Next rnd: K21 [19, 20, 22, 21, 22], turn.
Next row (WS): Sl1, k4, purl to end.
Raglan Dec Row: Sl1, p4, *knit to 2 sts before marker, k2tog, sl m, ssk; rep from * 3 more times, knit to end. 8 sts dec'd.
Maintaining 5 sts at beg and end of row in garter st with slipped st selvages as established, rep Raglan Dec Row on every 2nd row 9 [6, 4, 4, 3, 6] more times, then every 4th row 0 [1, 2, 3, 3, 1] times. 52 [52, 60, 64, 68, 68] sts rem: 11 [11, 13, 14, 14, 14] for each side of front, 22 [22, 26, 28, 28, 28] for back, and 4 [4, 4, 4, 6, 6] for each sleeve.
Work even if necessary until yoke measures 5.5 [6.25, 6.75, 7.25, 7.75, 8]"/14 [16, 17, 18.5, 19.5, 20.5]cm from underarm, ending with a WS row. BO all sts.

Hood

With MC and larger circular needle, RS facing, pick up and knit 52 [52, 60, 64, 68, 68] sts around neck edge.
Row 1 (WS): Sl1, k4, p15 [15, 18, 20, 21, 21], pm, p12 [12, 14, 14, 16, 16], pm, purl to end.
Row 2 (RS): Sl1, p4, knit to end.
Maintaining 5 sts at beg and end of row in garter st with slipped st selvages as established, work 3 [3, 5, 5, 5, 5] rows even.
Inc Row (RS): Sl1, p4, knit to marker, m1R, sl m, knit to marker, sl m, m1L, knit to end. 2 sts inc'd.
Rep Inc Row on every 6 [6, 8, 8, 8, 8]th row 5 [5, 6, 6, 7, 7] more times. 64 [64, 74, 78, 84, 84] sts.

Work even until hood measures 9 [10, 10, 11, 11, 12]"/23 [25.5, 25.5, 28, 28, 30.5]cm from pick-up row, ending with a WS row. Divide sts evenly over two needles. With right sides facing, join top of hood using a 3-needle BO.

FINISHING

Sew underarm seams. Weave in ends. Block.

ABOUT THE DESIGNER

After 13 years as a history professor, Elizabeth Green Musselman (elizabethgm on Ravelry) recently became a full-time knitting editor, designer, and teacher. She works primarily as art director and editor for Cooperative Press. Find her online at darkmatterknits.com.

RIB CHART

TREADS CHART

☐ Knit with MC

■ Knit with CC

• Purl with MC

☐ Pattern repeat

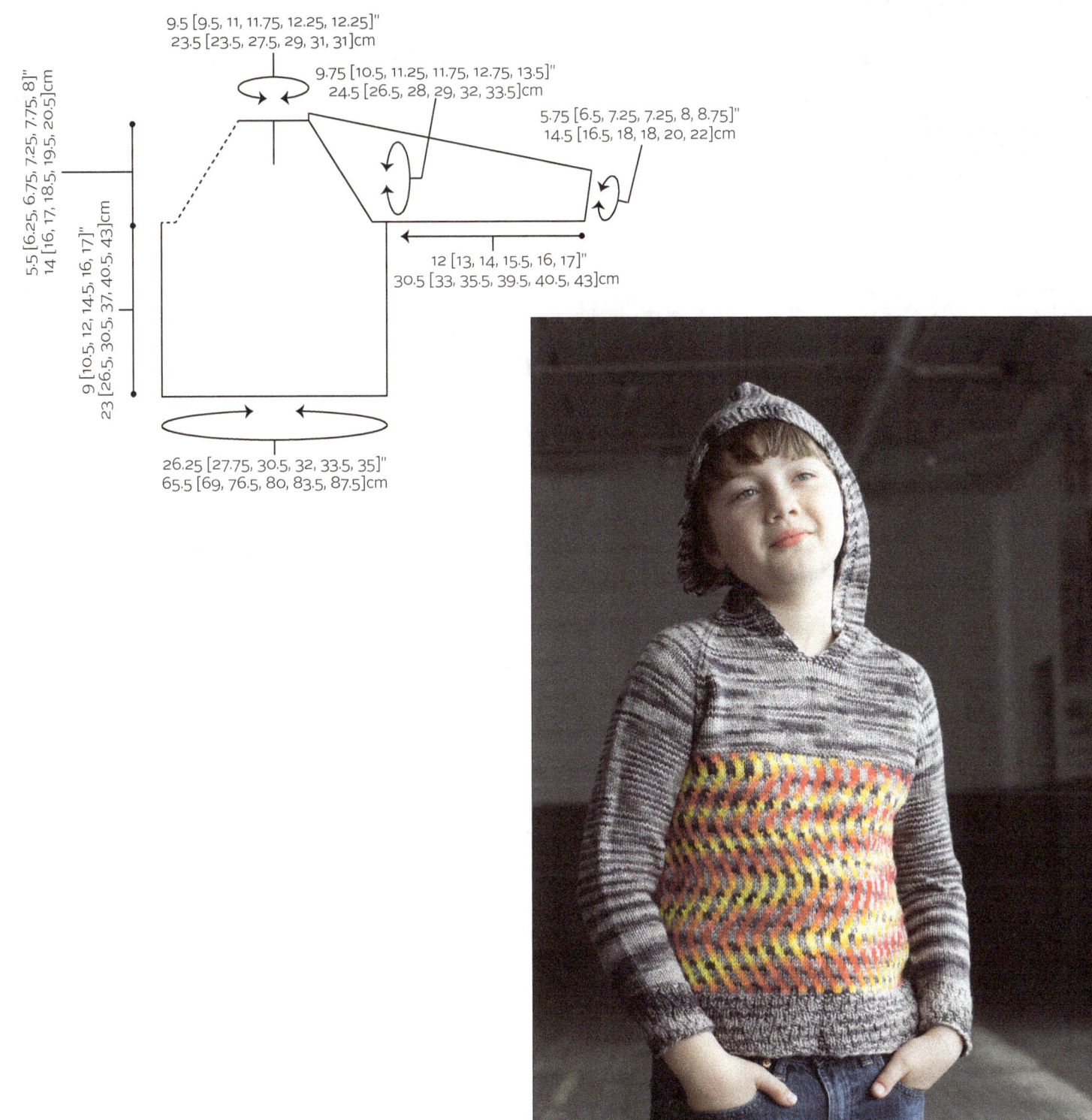

WEINIG WORTEL
BY ELLEN BOUCHER

DIFFICULTY

INTERMEDIATE

This whimsical hat, designed with my Dutch friend Judith, and her redhead husband in mind (the name means "little carrot" in Dutch and is pronounced *VINE-igg VOR-tull*), uses a surprisingly simple Estonian technique called vikkel braid to add texture to the finished result, and interest for the knitter.

SIZE
One size

FINISHED MEASUREMENTS
Circumference 16"/40.5cm

MATERIALS
[MC] Three Irish Girls Galenas Merino [100% merino wool; 220yd/201m per 100g skein]; color: Kieran; 1 skein
[CC] Curious Creek Fibers Kilimanjaro [95% mohair, 5% nyllon; 121yd/111m per 100g skein]; color: Tilting the Gizmo; 1 skein

Set of five US #5/3.75mm double-point needles

Yarn needle

GAUGE
18 sts/28 rows = 4"/10cm with MC in stockinette

STITCHES
I-cord:
Knit 1 row. *At end of row, do not turn work. Slide sts back to working end of dpn, draw yarn tightly across back of work, and knit row again.* Repeat from * to *.

Loopy I-cord (worked over 3 sts):
Work as for regular I-cord for 6 rows.
Next row: K1, [m1, make a loop by wrapping yarn around your finger, slip m1 from right needle to left, knit m1 tog with next st on left needle] twice.
Repeat these 7 rows.

PATTERN
Hat
With MC, CO 72 sts. Divide evenly over 4 needles (18 sts per needle) and join to work in the round.
Knit 8 rnds.

Vikkel Braid Rnd: M1, place st just made on left needle.
- Step 1: Knit second st on left needle tbl but do not slip off needle; knit first st on left needle, slip both first and second sts off left needle.
- Step 2: Transfer 1 st from right needle to left.
- Rep Steps 1–2 to end of rnd, ending with Step 1. At end of rnd, slip the first st of the next rnd from left needle to right, then pass second st on right needle over the slipped st to return to original number of sts.

Knit 6 rnds.
Rep Vikkel Braid Rnd.
Knit 5 rnds.
Rep Vikkel Braid Rnd.
Knit 5 rnds.

Vikkel Braid Dec Rnd: M1, place st just made on left needle.
- * Step 1: Knit second st on left needle tbl but do not slip off needle; knit first st on left needle, slip both first and second sts off left needle.
- Step 2: Transfer 1 st from right needle to left.
- Rep Steps 1–2 until 3 sts remain on left dpn. Knit second and third sts on left needle tog tbl, do not slip off needle; knit first st on left needle, slip first/second/third sts off left needle. 1 st dec'd. Transfer 1 st from right needle to next dpn. *
- Rep from * to * for each dpn, for a total of 4 sts dec'd. At end of round, do not transfer 1 st from right needle to left, but slip the first st of the next round from left needle

to right, then pass second st on right needle over the slipped st.

Knit 5 rnds.
Stockinette Dec Rnd: *Knit to last 2 sts on dpn, k2tog; rep from * 3 more times. 4 sts dec'd.
Knit 5 rnds.
Rep Vikkel Braid Dec Rnd.

Work the following 24 rnds three times—12 sts rem at end:
Knit 5 rnds.
Rep Vikkel Braid Dec Rnd.
Knit 5 rnds.
Rep Vikkel Braid Dec Rnd.
Knit 5 rnds.
Rep Stockinette Dec Rnd.
Knit 5 rnds.
Rep Vikkel Braid Dec Rnd.

Knit 2 rnds.
Rep Stockinette Dec Rnd. 8 sts rem.
Knit 2 rnds.
Next rnd: *K2tog; rep from * to end. 4 sts rem.

Work I-cord over rem sts for 1"/2.5cm. Break yarn, pull through rem sts and fasten off.

Leaves
Lay hat flat and mark center on each side. With CC, RS facing, pick up and knit 3 sts from bottom edge at center point, work Loopy I-cord for 4"/10cm, break yarn, pull through sts and fasten off. Pick up and knit 3 sts to left of first i-cord and repeat. Pick up and knit 3 sts to right of first i-cord and repeat. Turn hat over and work leaves to match on opposite side.

FINISHING
Weave in ends. Block.

ABOUT THE DESIGNER
Ellen inherited her knitting prowess from her Nan, Dorothy, and her Great Aunt Enid, who taught her as a girl. She lives, crafts and plays pretend in Wellington, New Zealand, with an awesome costume wardrobe and a perfectly reasonable, nay, austere, amount of yarn.

ELSIEBELLE SUNDRESS
BY HANNAH CUVIELLO

DIFFICULTY

INTERMEDIATE

This little summer dress is sweet and straightforward with just a touch of flounce.

SIZES
Approx age 12 mos. [18 mos., 24 mos., 3 yrs., 4 yrs.] (shown in size 18 mos.)

FINISHED MEASUREMENTS
Chest 20 [20.75, 21, 21.75, 22.75]"/50 [51.5, 52.5, 54, 56.5]cm

MATERIALS
[MC] Pico Accuardi Dyeworks Ultra Pima [100% pima cotton; 220yd/201m per 100g skein]; color: Savannah; 2 [2, 3, 3, 3] skeins
[CC] Pico Accuardi Dyeworks Ultra Pima; color: Walnut; 1 skein

24-inch US #4/3.5mm circular needle

Yarn needle
Stitch markers
2 large (skirt/pant type) hook and bar closures
Five or six ½"/13mm buttons

GAUGE
24 sts/32 rows = 4"/10cm in stockinette

PATTERN NOTES
The belt is worked first, then sts are picked up from the top edge and the bodice is worked flat. Sts are picked up from the bottom edge of the belt to work the skirt in the round.

Slip all stitches purlwise with yarn in front unless otherwise directed.

STITCHES
Brioche Mesh Stitch
(Worked in the rnd over an even number of sts. When working this stitch, slip all sts purlwise with yarn in back.)
Rnd 1 (set-up rnd): *P1, yo, sl1; rep from * to end.
Rnd 2 (set-up rnd): K1, *sl the yo, k2; rep from * to last 2 sts, sl the yo, k1.
Rnd 3: *Yo, sl1, p2tog (the slipped yo and the next st); rep from * to end.
Rnd 4: *Sl the yo, k2; rep from * to end.
Rnd 5: *P2tog (the slipped yo and the next st), yo, sl1; rep from * to end.
Rnd 6: K1, *sl the yo, k2; rep from * to last 2 sts, sl the yo, k1.
Rep Rnds 3–6 for pattern.

PATTERN
Belt
With CC, CO 144 [148, 150, 156, 162] sts. Do not join. Beg with a knit row, work in stockinette for 9 [11, 11, 11, 11] rows.

Next row (WS): Knit.
Next row (RS): K12 [12, 12, 13, 13], purl to last 12 [12, 12, 13, 13] sts, knit to end.

Beg with a purl row, work in stockinette for 8 [10, 10, 10, 10] more rows.

Joining row (WS): Fold fabric in half at the purl ridge. Pick up the first CO loop from the bottom edge of the work and place it on the left needle. K2tog (picked up loop and first st on needle). Pick up next CO loop and k2tog with the next st on needle. Pass second st on right needle over first to BO 1 st. Continue joining and binding off until 9 [9, 9, 10, 10] sts have been bound off. Continue joining without binding off until 3 [3, 3, 4, 4] sts rem, then join and BO the rem sts. Cut yarn. 132 [136, 138, 142, 148] sts.

Bodice
Turn your work so that the purl ridge created by the joining row is facing you. This is your RS. Join MC. Knit 1 row, dec 0 [1,

0, 1, 1] st. 132 [135, 138, 141, 147] sts. Work in stockinette for 13 [15, 15, 19, 23] more rows, ending with a WS row.

Divide for armholes (RS): K31 [32, 33, 33, 35], BO 6 sts, k54 [55, 56, 59, 61], BO 6 sts, k35 [36, 37, 37, 39].

Right back:
Work in stockinette over last group of 35 [36, 37, 37, 39] sts for 30 [32, 34, 38, 40] rows, ending with a RS row.
BO 24 [25, 26, 25, 27] sts at beg of next row. 11 [11, 11, 12, 12] sts. Work 1 RS row even.
Next row (WS): P5 [5, 7, 8, 8], turn.
Next row: Sl1, knit to end.

Sizes – [–, 24 mos., 3 yrs., 4 yrs.] only:
Next row (WS): P – [–, 4, 4, 4], turn.
Next row: Sl1, knit to end.

All sizes:
Next row (WS): Purl across all sts, closing gaps at turning point(s) as foll: purl to the gap, with right needle pick up the purl bump below the next st and place it on the left needle, ssp.
Place sts on holder.

Left back:
Join MC to first group of 31 [32, 33, 33, 35] sts with RS facing. Work in stockinette for 30 [32, 34, 38, 40] rows, ending with a WS row.
BO 20 [21, 22, 21, 23] sts at beg of next row. 11 [11, 11, 12, 12] sts. Work 1 WS row even.
Next row (RS): K5 [5, 7, 8, 8], turn.
Next row: Sl1, purl to end.

Sizes – [–, 24 mos., 3 yrs., 4 yrs.] only:
Next row (RS): K – [–, 4, 4, 4], turn.
Next row: Sl1, purl to end.

All sizes:
Next row (RS): Knit across all sts, closing gaps at turning point(s) as foll: knit to the gap, with right needle pick up the back of the st below the next and place it on the left needle, k2tog.
Place sts on holder.

Front:
Join MC to rem group of 54 [55, 56, 59, 61] sts with RS facing. Work in stockinette for 18 [20, 20, 24, 24] rows, ending with a WS row.
Next row (RS): K11 [11, 11, 12, 12], BO 32 [33, 34, 35, 37] sts, k11 [11, 11, 12, 12].

Right shoulder:
Work in stockinette over second group of 11 [11, 11, 12, 12] sts for 13 [13, 15, 15, 17] rows, ending with a WS row.
Next row (RS): K5 [5, 7, 8, 8], turn.
Next row: Sl1, purl to end.

Sizes – [–, 24 mos., 3 yrs., 4 yrs.] only:
Next row (RS): K – [–, 4, 4, 4], turn.
Next row: Sl1, purl to end.

All sizes:
Next row (RS): Knit across all sts, closing gaps at turning point(s) as foll: knit to the gap, with right needle pick up the back of the st below the next and place it on the left needle, k2tog.
Place sts on holder.

Left shoulder:
Join MC to rem 11 [11, 11, 12, 12] sts with RS facing. Work 13 [13, 15, 15, 17] rows stockinette, ending with a RS row.
Next row (WS): P5 [5, 7, 8, 8], turn.
Next row: Sl1, knit to end.

Sizes – [–, 24 mos., 3 yrs., 4 yrs.] only:
Next row (WS): P – [–, 4, 4, 4], turn.
Next row: Sl1, knit to end.

All sizes:
Next row (WS): Purl across all sts, closing gaps at turning point(s) as foll: purl to the gap, with right needle pick up the purl bump below the next st and place it on the left needle, ssp. Place sts on holder.

Skirt
With RS facing, using MC, pick up and knit 120 [124, 126, 130, 136] sts in the second row of purl bumps on the back side of the belt (not the purl ridge that forms the bottom of the belt). Pm and join to work in the round.
Next rnd: K20 [20, 21, 21, 22], pm, k20 [20, 21, 21, 22], pm, k40 [44, 42, 46, 48], pm, k20 [20, 21, 21, 22], pm, k20 [20, 21, 21, 22].
Continuing in stockinette, work 1 [2, 2, 2, 3] rnds even.
Inc Rnd: *Knit to 1 st before marker, m1, k1, sl m, m1; rep from * three more times, knit to end. 8 sts inc'd.
Rep Inc Rnd on every 2nd [3rd, 3rd, 3rd, 4th] rnd 7 [7, 7, 8, 8] more times. 184 [188, 190, 202, 208] sts.
Work even until skirt measures 2.25 [3.25, 4.75, 5.75, 7.75]"/5.5 [8, 12.5, 15, 19.5]cm from belt.
Cut MC. Join CC.
Knit 1 rnd. Purl 1 rnd. Knit 10 [12, 12, 12, 12] rnds. Purl 1 rnd.
Cut CC. Join MC.
Knit 1 rnd. Change to Brioche Mesh St and work even until skirt measures 6 [7.25, 9.5, 10.5, 12.75]"/15 [18, 24, 26.5, 32]cm from belt. BO loosely.

FINISHING
Join shoulders using a 3-needle BO.

Armhole edging:
Using CC, with RS facing, pick up and knit 6 sts from BO at base of armhole, then 30 [32, 34, 38, 40] more sts around armhole. Do not join.
Row 1 (WS): Knit.
Row 2 (RS): Use the backward loop method to CO 3 sts on left needle, (kfb) 3 times, turn.
Row 3: Sl1, k5.
Row 4: Sl1, k4, k2tog (1 st from edging and 1 picked-up st from armhole). Turn.
Row 5: Sl1, k5.
Row 6: Sl1, (yo, k2tog) twice, k2tog (1 st from edging and 1 from armhole). Turn.
Row 7: Sl1, (yo, k2tog) twice, k1.
Rep Rows 6–7 another 27 [29, 31, 35, 37] times, then Row 6 only once more.
Next row: (K2tog) 3 times.
Next row: Sl1, k2tog, psso, then BO the 6 underarm sts pwise.

Front neck edging:
Using CC, with RS facing, pick up and knit 22 [22, 23, 24, 26] sts along the front BO edge.
Row 1 (WS): Knit.
Row 2 (RS): Use the backward loop method to CO 6 sts on left needle, sl1, k4, k2tog (1 st from edging and 1 picked-up st from armhole). Turn.
Row 3: Sl1, k5.
Row 4: Sl1, (yo, k2tog) twice, k2tog (1 st from edging and 1 from armhole). Turn.
Row 5: Sl1, (yo, k2tog) twice, k1.
Rep Rows 4–5 another 19 [19, 20, 21, 23] times.
Next row: Sl1, k4, k2tog. Turn.
Next row: Sl1, k5.
BO all sts. Sew CO and BO edges to sides of neckline.

Left back neck edging:
Using CC, with RS facing, pick up and knit 13 [14, 15, 14, 16] sts along the left back BO edge.
Row 1 (WS): Knit.
Row 2 (RS): Use the backward loop method to CO 6 sts on left needle, sl1, k4, k2tog (1 st from edging and 1 picked-up st from armhole). Turn.
Row 3: Sl1, k5.
Row 4: Sl1, (yo, k2tog) twice, k2tog (1 st from edging and 1 from armhole). Turn.
Row 5: Sl1, (yo, k2tog) twice, k1.
Rep Rows 4–5 another 10 [11, 12, 11, 13] times.
Next row: Sl1, k4, k2tog. Turn.
Next row: Sl1, k5.
BO all sts. Sew BO edge to side of neckline.

Right back neck edging:
Using CC, with RS facing, pick up and knit 16 [17, 18, 17, 19] sts along right back BO edge.
Row 1 (WS): Knit.
Row 2 (RS): Use the backward loop method to CO 6 sts on left needle, sl1, k4, k2tog (1 st from edging and 1 picked-up st from armhole). Turn.
Row 3: Sl1, k5.
Row 4: Sl1, (yo, k2tog) twice, k2tog (1 st from edging and 1 from armhole). Turn.
Row 5: Sl1, (yo, k2tog) twice, k1.

Rep Rows 4–5 another 13 [14, 15, 14, 16] times.
Next row: Sl1, k4, k2tog. Turn.
Next row: Sl1, k5.
BO all sts. Sew CO edge to side of neckline.

Side neck edgings:
Using CC, with RS facing, pick up and knit 6 [6, 9, 9, 12] sts along side neck edge.
Row 1 (WS): Knit.
Row 2 (RS): Use the backward loop method to CO 6 sts on left needle, sl1, k4, k2tog (1 st from edging and 1 picked-up st from armhole). Turn.
Row 3: Sl1, k5.
Row 4: Sl1, (yo, k2tog) twice, k2tog (1 st from edging and 1 from armhole). Turn.
Row 5: Sl1, (yo, k2tog) twice, k1.
Rep Rows 4–5 another 3 [3, 6, 6, 9] times.
Next row: Sl1, k4, k2tog. Turn.
Next row: Sl1, k5.
BO all sts. Sew BO and CO edges to top of back and front neck edgings.

Buttonhole band:
Using CC, with RS facing, pick up and knit 3 sts for every 4 rows along left back edge (including neck edging).
Row 1 (WS): Knit.
Place 4 or 5 evenly spaced markers for buttonholes.
Row 2 (RS): *Knit to 1 st before marker, BO 2 sts; rep from * 3 or 4 more times, knit to end.
Row 3: *Knit to BO sts, use the cable method to CO 2 sts; rep from * 3 or 4 more times, knit to end.
BO all sts.

Weave in ends. Block. Sew buttons to right back, adjusting placement to best fit your child; buttons can be moved to give more room as the child grows. Sew hook and bar closures to belt, having one hook on WS of left belt tab, and other hook on RS of right belt tab; place bars to correspond. Sew the remaining button to the RS of the left belt tab, on top of hook.

Using scraps of MC and CC, embroider lazy daisies on one side of skirt as shown in photo.

ABOUT THE DESIGNER
Hannah Cuviello (hannahcuv on Ravelry) does not remember a time when yarn was not a huge part of her life. Lately, it has been even more so as she and her family run their online yarn store, Abundant Yarn Online (www.abundant-yarn.com).

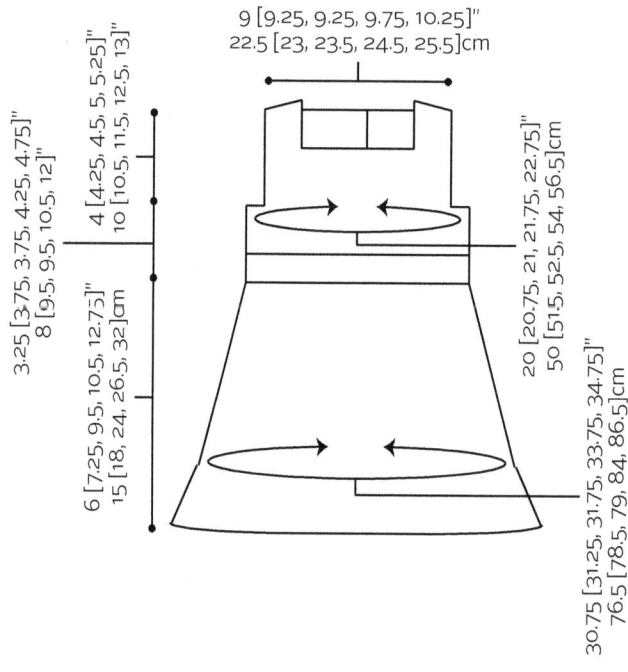

SUPERKID SWEATER

BY HANNAH INGALLS

DIFFICULTY

INTERMEDIATE

This colorful sweater will let your child feel like a mighty superhero. The pattern includes several emblem options worked in simple intarsia, and also features a dashing cape, which snaps in place for safety and versatility.

During the photo shoot, the model for this sweater declared himself Rocket Ship Boy, and once he had his cape snapped on, we could barely get him to stop running long enough to take his photo. Poor Rocket Ship Boy cried balefully when he had to take the garment off—even though the temperature was 85 degrees!

SIZES
2 [4, 6, 8] (shown in size 4)

FINISHED MEASUREMENTS
Chest 24 [25.5, 27, 29]"/60 [64, 68, 72]cm

MATERIALS
Stitch Jones Dyepot Worsted [100% superwash merino; 218yds/199m per 100g skein]

- [MC] Saffron; 2 [2, 3, 3] skeins
- [CC1] Delft; 1 [1, 1, 1] skein
- [CC2] Forest; 1 [1, 1, 1] skein

Set of US #7/4.5mm double-point needles
US #7/4.5mm straight needles

Yarn needle
Stitch markers
Bobbins for intarsia (optional)
Two sew-on snaps, size 4
Embroidery floss in colors to match MC and CC2
Large sewing needle

GAUGE
20 sts/28 rows = 4"/10cm in stockinette

STITCHES
2x2 Rib (multiple of 4 sts + 2):
Row 1 (WS): *P2, k2; rep from * to last 2 sts, p2.
Row 2 (RS): *K2, p2; rep from * to last 2 sts, k2.
Rep Rows 1–2.

Seed Stitch (odd number of sts):
Row 1: K1, *p1, k1; rep from * to end.
Rep Row 1.

PATTERN NOTES
This sweater is worked flat in pieces and seamed. The front motif is worked using the intarsia method, as is the color blocking on the cape. When changing colors, make sure to bring the new yarn up from underneath the old, which will twist the strands together and prevent a hole from forming.

PATTERN
Back
With MC and straight needles, CO 62 [66, 70, 74] sts. Work in 2x2 Rib for 1"/2.5cm, ending with a WS row. Change to stockinette stitch and work even until piece measures 6 [7, 9, 11]"/15.5 [18, 23, 27]cm from CO, ending with a WS row.
BO 5 sts at beg of next 2 rows. 52 [56, 60, 64] sts.

Raglan shaping:
Dec row (RS): K1, ssk, work to last 3 sts, k2tog, k1. 2 sts dec'd.
Work 1 row even.
Rep the last 2 rows 13 [14, 15, 16] more times. 24 [26, 28, 30] sts.
BO all sts.

Front
Work same as back until piece measures 6 [7, 9, 11]"/15.5 [18, 23, 28]cm from CO, ending with a WS row.

Raglan shaping and intarsia:
Next row (RS): BO 5 sts, knit to end.
Next row (WS): BO 5 sts, purl until there are 16 [18, 20, 22] sts on right needle, pm, p20, pm, purl to end. 52 [56, 60, 64] sts.
Beginning on next row, work Rows 1–24 of Planet, Rocket, Star, or Shield chart between markers, then remove markers and continue with MC over all sts. AT THE SAME TIME, work raglan shaping as for back. 24 [26, 28, 30] sts.
BO all sts.

Sleeves
With MC and straight needles, CO 34 [38, 38, 38] sts. Work in 2x2 Rib for 1"/2.5cm, ending with a WS row. Change to stockinette stitch and work 2 rows even.
Inc row (RS): K1, m1, knit to last st, m1, k1. 2 sts inc'd.
Rep Inc Row on every 6th row 6 [6, 7, 8] more times. 48 [52, 54, 56] sts.
Work even until piece measures 10 [11, 12, 13]"/25.5 [28, 30.5, 33]cm from CO, ending with a WS row.
BO 5 sts at beg of next 2 rows. 38 [42, 44, 46] sts.
Dec row (RS): K1, ssk, knit to last 3 sts, k2tog, k1. 2 sts dec'd.
Work 1 row even.
Rep the last 2 rows 13 [14, 15, 16] more times. 10 [12, 12, 12] sts.
BO all sts.

Cape
With CC2 and straight needles, CO 63 [67, 71, 75] sts. Work in Seed St for 1"/2.5cm, ending with a WS row.
Begin working body of cape in intarsia as foll:
Row 1 (RS): With CC2, work 6 sts in Seed St; with CC1, k1, ssk, knit to last 9 sts, k2tog, k1; with CC2, work 6 sts in Seed St. 2 sts dec'd.
Row 2 (WS): With CC2, work 6 sts in Seed St; with CC1, purl to last 6 sts; with CC2, work 6 sts in Seed St.
Row 3: With CC2, work 6 sts in Seed st; with CC1, knit to last 6 sts; with CC2, work 6 sts in Seed st.
Row 4: Rep Row 2.
Rep Rows 1–4 another 15 [16, 17, 18] times. 31 [33, 35, 37] sts.
Break CC1 and continue with CC2 only.

■ RS: knit with MC; WS: purl with MC

■ RS: knit with CC1; WS: purl with CC1

■ RS: knit with CC2; WS: purl with CC2

PLANET CHART

ROCKET CHART

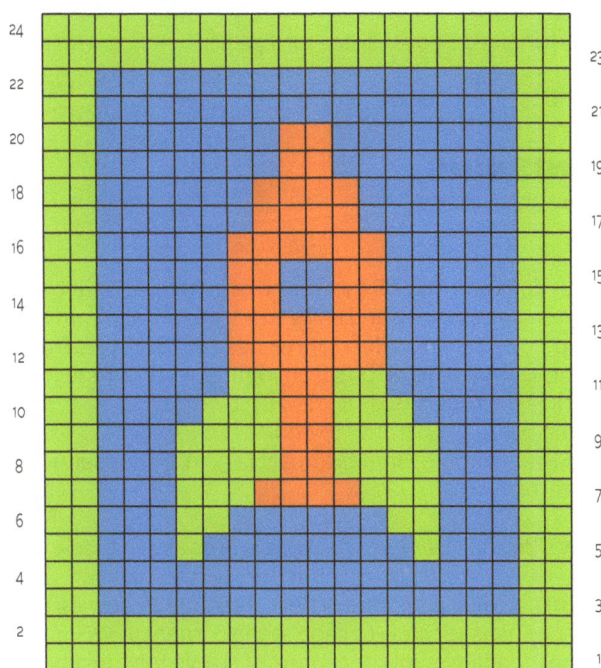

STAR CHART

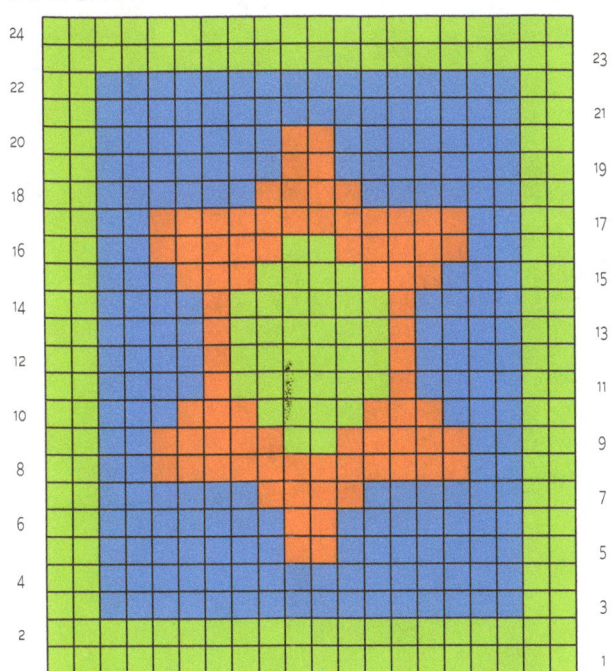

SHIELD CHART

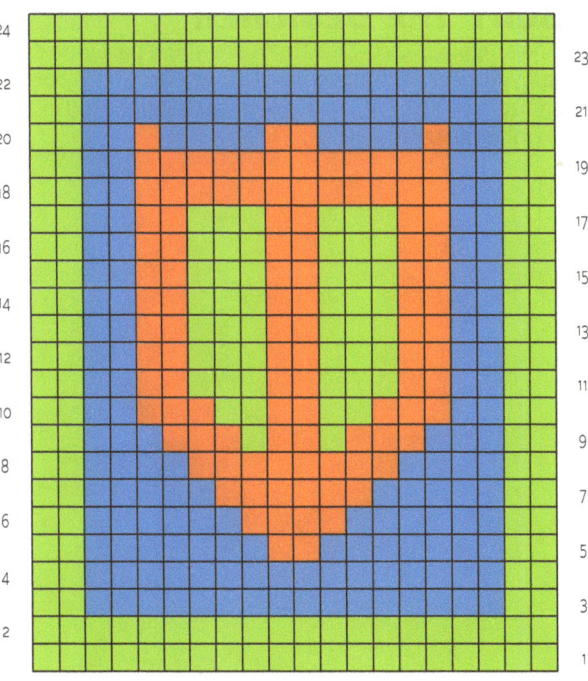

Next row (RS): Work 6 sts in Seed st, knit to last 6 sts, work 6 sts in Seed st.
Work in Seed St over all sts for 1"/2.5cm, ending with a WS row.
BO loosely in pattern.

FINISHING
Sew raglan seams.

Collar:
With dpns and MC, RS facing and beginning at right back raglan seam, pick up and knit 22 [24, 26, 28] sts from back, 8 [10, 10, 10] sts from left sleeve, 22 [24, 26, 28] sts from front, and 8 [10, 10, 10] sts from right sleeve. Pm and join to work in the round. 60 [68, 72, 76] sts.
Rnd 1: *K2, p2; rep from * to end.
Rep Rnd 1 until collar measures 1"/2.5cm. BO loosely in pattern.

Sew side and sleeve seams. Weave in ends and block.

With matching embroidery floss threaded on sewing needle, attach snaps securely to cape at top corners of WS, and to corresponding points at centers of sleeve tops, just below collar.

ABOUT THE DESIGNER
Hannah Ingalls lives in Seattle where she is part yarn store employee, part nanny, and part Norwegian. She is one of the organizers of Knit Fit!, a fiber festival that debuted in November 2012.

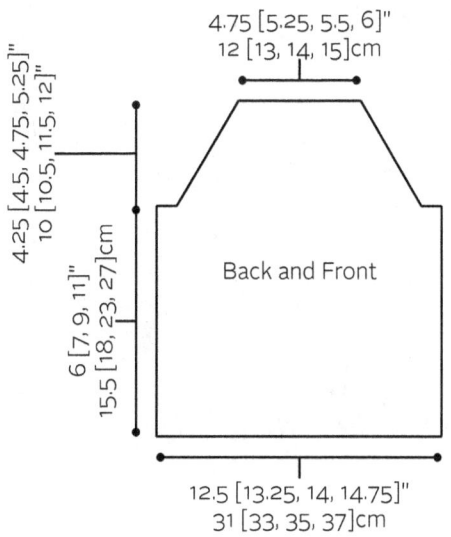
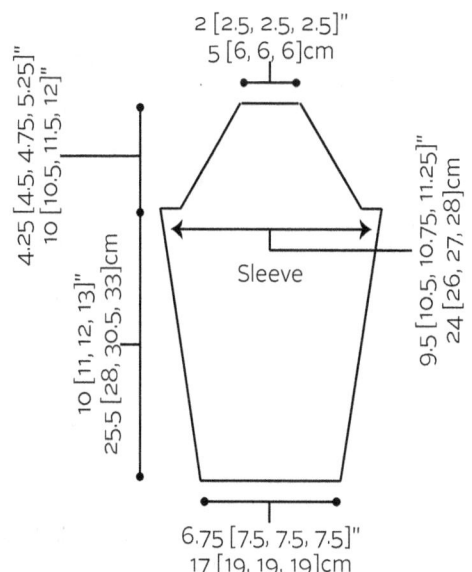
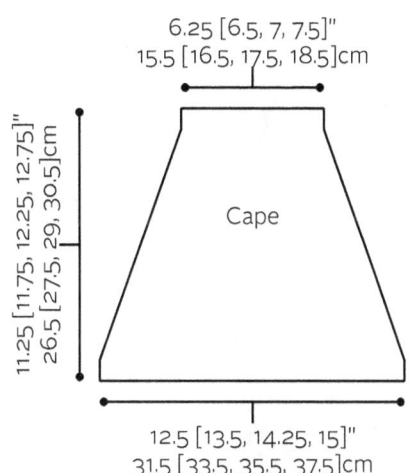

PETAL BONNET
BY KOURTNEY ROBINSON

DIFFICULTY

INTERMEDIATE

All babies make me think of flower buds, and the unique edging on this top-down bonnet makes lovely "petals" to frame a little face.

SIZES
Approximate age preemie [newborn, 3 mos., 6 mos., 1 year] (shown in 6 mos. size)
Babies' head sizes vary greatly. If in doubt, make the next size up—babies grow!

FINISHED MEASUREMENTS
Length around face opening (from tie to tie) 8 [9, 9.75, 10.5, 11.25]"/20 [22.5, 24.5, 26.5, 28]cm

MATERIALS
Gray version:
Schoppel-Wolle Cashmere Queen [45% merino, 35% cashmere, 20% silk; 153yds/140m per 50g skein]
- [MC] Color 1144 7873; 1 skein
- [CC] Color 1144 7130; 1 skein

32-inch US #5/3.75mm circular needle

Green version:
Louet Gems Sport [100% merino wool; 225yds/205m per 100g skein]
- [MC] Willow; 1 skein
- [CC] Aqua; 1 skein

Schulana Kid-Seta [70% kid mohair, 30% silk; 231 yds/210m per 25g skein]; color: 6 8119; 1 skein (held double with MC & CC in green version)

32-inch US #3/3.25mm circular needle

Both versions:
Stitch markers
Yarn needle
Crochet hook

GAUGE
22 sts/32 rows = 4"/10cm in stockinette

PATTERN NOTES
Bonnet is worked from the crown outwards, in the round, beginning with a double-sided cast on (such as is often used on socks knit from the toe up). I prefer Judy's Magic Cast On (www.persistentillusion.com/blogblog/techniques/magic-cast-on/magic-cast-on-2), but you can use the Figure 8 or Turkish (also called Eastern) cast on (knittingdaily.com/blogs/daily/archive/2008/07/28/exploring-a-tricky-cast-on-for-toe-up-socks.aspx).

Pattern is written for the Magic Loop method on one long circular needle.

PATTERN
Crown
With MC and a double-sided cast on (see Pattern Notes), CO 32 [36, 40, 44, 44] sts (16 [18, 20, 22, 22] sts on each needle tip).

Rnd 1: K1, pm, k14 [16, 18, 20, 20], pm, k1; k1, pm, k7 [8, 9, 10, 10], pm, k7 [8, 9, 10, 10], pm, k1.
Rnd 2: K1, sl m, m1R, knit to next marker, m1L, sl m, k1; k1, sl m, m1R, knit to next marker, sl m, knit to next marker, m1L, sl m, k1. 4 sts inc'd.
Rnd 3: Knit.
Rep Rnds 2–3 another 5 [7, 8, 9, 10] times, then Row 2 only once. 60 [72, 80, 88, 92] sts; that is, 30 [36, 40, 44, 46] on each needle tip.

Nape shaping:
Rnd 1: K1, sl m, m1R, knit to next marker, m1L, sl m, k1; k1, sl m, m1R, knit to 3 sts before next marker, ssk, k1, sl m, k1, k2tog, knit to next marker, m1L, sl m, k1. 2 sts inc'd.
Rnd 2: Knit.
Rep Rnds 1–2 another 2 [2, 2, 2, 3] times. 66 [78, 86, 94, 100] sts; that is, 36 [42, 46, 50, 54] sts on needle 1 and 30 [36, 40, 44, 46] sts on needle 2.

Brim set-up:
Rnd 1: K1, sl m, m1R, k1 [1, 0, 2, 1], (yo, k2tog, k4) 5 [6, 7, 7, 8] times, yo, k2tog, k1 [1, 0, 2, 1], m1L, sl m, k1; k1, sl m, m1R, knit to 3 sts before next marker, ssk, k1, sl m, k1, k2tog, knit to next marker, m1L, sl m, k1. 68 [80, 88, 96, 102] sts.
Rnd 2: Knit.
Rnd 3: K1, sl m, m1R, knit to next marker, m1L, sl m, k1; k3 [2, 4, 2, 3] removing marker, *p2, k2; rep from * to 4 sts before next marker, p1, p2tog, k1, remove marker, k1, p2tog, p1, *k2, p2; rep from * to last 3 [2, 4, 2, 3] sts, knit to end removing marker. 68 [80, 88, 96, 102] sts.
Rnd 4: Knit sts on needle 1; on needle 2, k3 [2, 4, 2, 3], p2, *k2, p2; rep from * to last 3 [2, 4, 2, 3] sts, knit to end.
Rnd 5: K1, sl m, m1R, knit to next marker, m1L, sl m, k1; k3 [2, 4, 2, 3], p2, *k2, p2; rep from * to last 3 [2, 4, 2, 3] sts, knit to end. 2 sts inc'd.
Rnd 6: Rep Rnd 4.
Rnd 7: Rep Rnd 5.
Rnd 8: Rep Rnd 4. 72 [84, 92, 100, 106] sts; that is, 44 [50, 54, 58, 62] sts on needle 1 and 28 [34, 38, 42, 44] sts on needle 2.

Contrast edging:
Change to CC.
Knit 1 rnd over all sts, removing remaining markers.
Next rnd: BO first 3 [3, 2, 4, 3] sts kwise. Work looped BO as follows: *With right needle, pull up a loop of yarn through yo hole 9 rnds below. Knit next st on left needle. Adjust tension on loop if necessary. Pass loop over st just knit. Pass second st on right needle over first to BO 1 st. Knit next st on left needle. Pass second st on right needle over first to BO 1 st.* Repeat from * to *, pulling up 3 loops in each yo hole, until 4 [4, 3, 5, 4] sts rem on needle 1. BO all rem sts kwise.

FINISHING
Weave in ends. Cut six 24"/60cm lengths of CC. Using crochet hook and three strands held together, pull up a loop through corner of bonnet (where break between needles 1 & 2 occurred) and draw strands through. Braid tightly, knot end, and trim.

Wash with wool wash and block gently over a little ball or a balloon, gently encouraging the "petal" edges to lie flat.

ABOUT THE DESIGNER
Kourtney Robinson is endlessly inspired by color, shape, and texture. She loves that knitting fits into the spare space and time between her darling girls and everything else. Find Kourtney online at dollybirdworkshop.com, and on Ravelry as mrsrobinson.

JACK & CLARA WINTRY ENSEMBLE

BY PEGGY BUMGARDNER

DIFFICULTY
INTERMEDIATE

Jack and Clara are boy and girl versions of snug earflap hats with adjustable chin straps and matching mitts and mittens. Cables and texture feature on the boyish set, while eyelets and lace adorn the feminine set. Thumbless mitts are perfect for tiny hands; the larger mittens have thumbs.

SIZES
Approximate age preemie [newborn, 6 mos., 12 mos., toddler] (shown in 6 mos. size)

FINISHED MEASUREMENTS
Jack hat circumference 11.25 [12.75, 16, 17.5, 19.25]"/28 [32, 40, 44, 48]cm
Clara hat circumference 10.5 [12, 16, 18.5, 20]"/26 [30, 40, 46, 50]cm
Mitt/mitten circumference 2.75 [4, 4.5, 5, 5]"/6.5 [10, 11.5, 12.5, 12.5]cm

MATERIALS
JACK ENSEMBLE:
[MC] A Verb for Keeping Warm Annapurna [80% superwash merino, 10% cashmere, 10% nylon; 385yd/352m per 113g skein]; color: Mermaid; 1 skein
[CC] A Verb for Keeping Warm Captivate [75% superwash merino, 15% silk, 10% cashmere; 385yd/352m per 113g skein]; color: Fortuna; 1 skein
Note: 1 skein of each yarn will make both the hat and mittens with yarn to spare

One ½"/13mm button

CLARA ENSEMBLE:
[MC] A Verb for Keeping Warm Annapurna; color: Le Cirque; 1 skein
[CC] A Verb for Keeping Warm Captivate; color: Brick; 1 skein
Note: 1 skein of each yarn will make both the hat and mittens with yarn to spare

Two ½"/13mm buttons

BOTH VERSIONS:
16-inch US #2/2.75mm circular needle
Set of US #2/2.75mm double-point needles
Yarn needle
Stitch markers
Stitch holder
Cable needle (cn)

GAUGE
30 sts/44 rnds = 4"/10cm in stockinette
30 sts/42 rnds = 4"/10cm in Mock Cable Rib
30 sts/44 rnds = 4"/10cm in Eyelet Rib

STITCHES
RT (right twist): Knit second st on left needle tbl but do not drop from needle, then knit first st on left needle and drop both sts.

Seed Stitch (worked in the round over an even number of sts)
Rnd 1: *K1, p1; rep from * to end.
Rnd 2: *P1, k1; rep from * to end.
Rep Rnds 1–2.

3x3 Rib (worked in the round over a multiple of 6 sts)
Rnd 1: *K3, p3; rep from * to end.
Rep Rnd 1.

Mock Cable Rib (worked in the round over a multiple of 6 sts)
Rnds 1–3: *P1, k2, p3; rep from * to end.
Rnd 4: *P1, RT, p3; rep from * to end.
Rep Rnds 1–4.

Eyelet Rib (worked in the round over a multiple of 6 sts)
Rnd 1: *K3, yo, p3; rep from * to end.
Rnd 2: *K4, p3; rep from * to end.
Rnd 3: *K1, k2tog, yo, k1, p3; rep from * to end.
Rnd 4: *K2, k2tog, p3; rep from * to end.
Rnd 5: *K1, yo, k2tog, p3; rep from * to end.
Rnd 6: *K3, p3; rep from * to end.
Rep Rnds 1–6.

I-cord:
Knit 1 row. *At end of row, do not turn work. Slide sts back to working end of dpn, draw yarn tightly across back of work, and knit row again.* Rep from * to *.

PATTERN
JACK HAT
Right Chin Strap and Earflap:
With CC, CO 5 [5, 7, 7, 7] sts.
Work in garter st, slipping the first st of each row, for 3 [4, 6, 6, 6] rows.
Buttonhole row: Sl1, k1 [1, 2, 2, 2], yo, k2tog, knit to end.
Rep the last 4 [5, 7, 7, 7] rows 2 [2, 3, 3, 3] more times.
Continue in garter st, slipping the first st of each row, for 3 [4, 4, 8, 10] more rows.

Sizes preemie [newborn] only:
Next row: Sl1, m1, k3, m1, k1. 7 [7] sts.
Next row: Sl1, knit to end.

All sizes:
Work Rows 1–13 [1–13, 1–26, 1–26, 1–26] of Jack Earflap chart. 21 [21, 31, 31, 31] sts. Place sts on a holder.

Left Chin Strap and Earflap:
With CC, CO 5 [5, 7, 7, 7] sts.
Work in garter st, slipping the first st of each row, for 15 [19, 32, 36, 38] rows.

Sizes preemie [newborn] only:
Next row: Sl1, m1, k3, m1, k1. 7 [7] sts.
Next row: Sl1, knit to end.

All sizes:
Work Rows 1–13 [1–13, 1–26, 1–26, 1–26] of Jack Earflap chart. 21 [21, 31, 31, 31] sts. Place sts on a holder.

Hat Body:
With circular needle and CC, use the backward loop method to CO 18 [24, 26, 30, 36] sts; with RS facing knit the 21 [21, 31, 31, 31] sts of left earflap, CO 24 [30, 32, 40, 46] sts, with RS facing knit the 21 [21, 31, 31, 31] sts of right earflap. Pm and join to work in the round. 84 [96, 120, 132, 144] sts.
Work in Seed St for 4 [6, 8, 10, 10] rnds.
Change to MC. Work Rnds 1–4 of Mock Cable Rib 2 [4, 6, 7, 8] times, then Rnds 1–3 only once.

Crown shaping:
Change to dpns when necessary.
Rnd 1 (dec rnd): *P1, RT, p1, p2tog; rep from * to end. 70 [80, 100, 110, 120] sts.
Rnds 2–4: *P1, k2, p2; rep from * to end.

Sizes – [newborn, 6 mos., 12 mos., toddler] only:
Rnd 5: *P1, RT, p2; rep from * to end.
Rnds 6–8: *P1, k2, p2; rep from * to end.
Rep Rnds 5–8 – [0, 0, 1, 1] more time(s).

All sizes:
Dec rnd: *P1, RT, p2tog; rep from * to end. 56 [64, 80, 88, 96] sts.
Next rnd: *P1, k2, p1; rep from * to end.
Rep last rnd 6 times more.
Dec rnd: Remove marker, p1, pm, *RT, p2tog; rep from * to end. 42 [48, 60, 66, 72] sts.
Next rnd: *K2, p1; rep from * to end.
Rep last rnd 0 [0, 0, 1, 1] more time(s).
Dec rnd: *K2tog, p1; rep from * to end. 28 [32, 40, 44, 48] sts.
Next rnd: *K1, p1; rep from * to end.
Rep last rnd 0 [0, 0, 1, 1] more time(s).
Dec rnd: *K2tog, rep from * to end. 14 [16, 20, 22, 24] sts.
Knit 1 [1, 1, 2, 2] rnds.
Dec rnd: *K2tog; rep from * to end. 7 [8, 10, 11, 12] sts.

Cut yarn, leaving a 12"/30cm tail. Thread through rem sts but do not pull closed yet.

Tassel:
Cut six strands of CC 6 [6, 8, 10, 10]"/15.5 [15.5, 20.5, 25.5, 25.5]cm long. Braid, using 2 strands held together. Knot each end and trim, leaving ½"/1.5cm ends. Repeat twice more. Tie all three braids together at center and sew center to inside of hat. Pull top of hat closed around base of tassel and fasten off.

Weave in ends. Block. Sew button to chin strap.

CLARA HAT
Right Chin Strap and Earflap:
With CC, CO 4 [4, 5, 5, 5] sts.
Row 1: Knit.
Row 2: Use the backward loop method to CO 1 [1, 2, 2, 2] sts, BO 1 [1, 2, 2, 2] sts, knit to end.
Rows 3–5: Rep Row 2.
Row 7 (buttonhole row): CO 1 [1, 2, 2, 2] sts, BO 1 [1, 2, 2, 2] sts, k0 [0, 1, 1, 1], yo, k2tog, k1.
Rep Rows 2–7 0 [1, 2, 3, 4] more times, then rep Row 2 only 6 [2, 6, 14, 10] times.
Next row (WS): Knit, inc 3 [3, 2, 2, 2] sts evenly spaced. 7 sts.
Work Rows 1–10 [1–10, 1–26, 1–26, 1–26] of Clara Earflap chart. 17 [17, 31, 31, 31] sts. Break yarn and place sts on holder.

Left Chin Strap and Earflap:
With CC, CO 4 [4, 5, 5, 5] sts.
Row 1: Knit.
Row 2: Use the backward loop method to CO 1 [1, 2, 2, 2] sts, BO 1 [1, 2, 2, 2] sts, knit to end.
Rep Row 2 another 11 [13, 29, 39, 39] times.
Next row (WS): Knit, inc 3 [3, 2, 2, 2] sts evenly spaced. 7 sts.
Work Rows 1–10 [1–10, 1–26, 1–26, 1–26] of Clara Earflap chart. 17 [17, 31, 31, 31] sts. Break yarn and place sts on holder.

Hat Body:
With circular needle and CC, use the backward loop method to CO 20 [26, 26, 34, 38] sts, with RS facing knit the 17 [17, 31, 31, 31] sts of left earflap, CO 24 [30, 32, 42, 50] sts, with RS facing knit the 17 [17, 31, 31, 31] sts of right earflap, pm and join to work in the round. 78 [90, 120, 138, 150] sts.
Next rnd: *K3, p3; rep from * to end.
Rep last rnd 2 [3, 7, 8, 9] more times.
Change to MC. Work Rnds 1–6 of Eyelet Rib 1 [2, 3, 4, 5] times.

Crown shaping:
Change to dpns when necessary.
Rnd 1: *K3, yo, p2tog, p1; rep from * to end.
Rnd 2: *K4, p2; rep from * to end.
Rnd 3: *K1, k2tog, yo, k1, p2; rep from * to end.
Rnd 4 (dec rnd): *K2, k2tog, p2; rep from * to end. 65 [75, 100, 115, 125] sts.
Rnd 5: *K1, yo, k2tog, p2; rep from * to end.
Rnd 6: *K3, p2; rep from * to end.
Rnd 7 (dec rnd): *K1, k2tog, p2; rep from * to end. 52 [60, 80, 92, 100] sts.
Rnd 8: *K2, p2; rep from * to end.

Rnd 9: *RT, p2; rep from * to end.
Rnd 10: *K2, p2; rep from * to end.
Rep Rnd 10 1 [2, 2, 3, 3] more times.
Next rnd: *RT, p2; rep from * to end.
Next rnd: *K2, p2; rep from * to end.
Rep the last rnd 0 [1, 1, 2, 3] more time(s).
Next rnd: *RT, p2; rep from * to end.
Next rnd: *K2, p2; rep from * to end.
Rep the last rnd 0 [1, 1, 1, 1] more time(s).
Dec rnd: *K2, p2tog; rep from * to end. 39 [45, 60, 69, 75] sts.
Next rnd: *RT, p1; rep from * to end.
Next rnd: *K2, p1; rep from * to end.
Dec rnd: *K2tog, p1; rep from * to end. 26 [30, 40, 46, 50] sts.
Next rnd: *K1, p1; rep from * to end.
Dec rnd: *Sl1, p1, psso; rep from * to end. 13 [15, 20, 23, 25] sts.
Knit 1 [1, 2, 2, 2] rnds.
Dec rnd: K1 [1, 0, 1, 1], *sl1, k1, psso; rep from * to end. 7 [8, 10, 12, 13] sts.
Cut yarn, thread tail through rem sts, pull closed, and fasten off.

Flower:
With CC and dpns, CO 3 sts. Make a 10"/25.5cm i-cord. Form into two figure-8s plus one extra loop, securing at center of each twist. Secure all centers together. Add button and sew to top of hat.

Weave in ends. Block. Sew button to chin strap.

JACK MITTS
(no thumbs; sizes preemie [newborn, 6 mos.])

With CC and dpns, CO 24 [36, 42] sts. Pm and join to work in the round. Work Rnds 1–4 of Mock Cable Rib 1 [2, 3] times.

Sizes preemie [newborn] only:
Next rnd: *P1, k2, p2tog, p1; rep from * to end. 20 [30] sts.

Size 6 mos. only:
Next rnd: (P1, k2, p2tog, p1) 6 times, p1, k2, p2tog, sl 1, remove marker, return slipped st to left needle, p2tog, pm. 34 sts.

All sizes:
Change to MC. Work in Seed St for 2 [4, 4] rnds.
**Change to stockinette and work 8 [12, 21] rnds even.
Dec rnd: K1, k2tog, k4 [9, 11], ssk, k1, pm, k1, k2tog, knit to last 3 sts, ssk, k1. 16 [26, 30] sts.
Knit 1 rnd.

Dec rnd: K1, k2tog, knit to 3 sts before marker, ssk, k1, sl m, k1, k2tog, knit to last 3 sts, ssk, k1. 4 sts dec'd.
Knit 1 rnd.
Rep the last 2 rnds 0 [2, 3] more times. 12 [14, 14] sts.
Divide rem sts evenly over 2 needles and graft together with Kitchener st.

Weave in ends. Block.

CLARA MITTS
(no thumbs; sizes preemie [newborn, 6 mos.])

With CC and dpns, CO 24 [36, 42] sts. Pm and join to work in the round. Work Rnds 1–4 of Mock Cable Rib 1 [2, 3] times.

Sizes preemie [newborn] only:
Next rnd: *P1, k2, p2tog, p1; rep from * to end. 20 [30] sts.

Size 6 mos. only:
Next rnd: (P1, k2, p2tog, p1) 6 times, p1, k2, p2tog, sl 1, remove marker, return slipped st to left needle, p2tog, pm. 34 sts.

All sizes:
Change to MC.
Next rnd: *K2tog, yo; rep from * to end.
Knit 1 rnd.
Rep the last 2 rnds 0 [1, 1] more time(s).

Complete as for Jack Mitts beginning at **.

JACK MITTENS
(sizes 12 mos. [toddler])

With CC and dpns, CO 48 [48] sts. Pm and join to work in the round. Work Rnds 1–4 of Mock Cable Rib 3 [4] times.
Next rnd: *P1, k2, p2tog, p1; rep from * to end. 40 [40] sts.

Change to MC. Work in Seed St for 6 [8] rnds.

**Thumb gusset:
Rnds 1, 3, 5, 7, 9, 11, 13: Knit.
Rnd 2: K1, m1L, knit to last st, m1R, k1. 42 [42] sts.
Rnd 4: K2, m1L, knit to last 2 sts, m1R, k2. 44 [44] sts.
Rnd 6: K3, m1L, knit to last 3 sts, m1R, k3. 46 [46] sts.
Rnd 8: K4, m1L, knit to last 4 sts, m1R, k4. 48 [48] sts.
Rnd 10: K5, m1L, knit to last 5 sts, m1R, k5. 50 [50] sts.
Rnd 12: K6, m1, knit to last 6 sts, m1R, k6. 52 [52] sts.
Rnd 14: Knit to last 7 sts, place next 14 sts on holder, pm for beg of rnd. 38 [38] sts.

Knit 10 [14] rnds.
Dec rnd: K1, k2tog, k13 [13], ssk, k1, pm, k2tog, knit to last 3 sts, ssk, k1. 34 [34] sts.
Knit 1 rnd.
Dec rnd: K1, k2tog, knit to 3 sts before marker, ssk, k1, pm, k1, k2tog, knit to last 3 sts, ssk, k1. 4 sts dec'd.
Knit 1 rnd.
Rep the last 2 rnds 3 [3] more times. 18 sts.
Divide rem sts evenly over 2 needles and graft together with Kitchener st.

Thumb:
Place the 14 held sts onto dpns. Join MC, knit across, pick up and knit 3 sts across gap. 17 sts.
Knit 5 [7] rnds.
Dec rnd: [K6, k2tog] twice, k1. 15 sts.
Knit 6 [8] rnds.
Dec rnd: [K3, k2tog] 3 times. 12 sts.
Dec rnd: *K2tog; rep from * to end. 6 sts.
Cut yarn, thread through rem sts, pull closed and fasten off.

Weave in ends. Block.

Loops (optional):
With CC, RS facing, pick up and knit 3 sts from side of cuff.
Work i-cord for 1.5"/4cm. BO and sew end to beginning.

CLARA MITTENS
(sizes 12 mos. [toddler])

With CC and dpns, CO 48 [48] sts. Pm and join to work in the round. Work Rnds 1–4 of Mock Cable Rib 3 [4] times.
Next rnd: *P1, k2, p2tog, p1; rep from * to end. 40 [40] sts.

Change to MC.
Next rnd: *K2tog, yo; rep from * to end.
Knit 1 rnd.
Rep the last 2 rnds 3 [4] more times.
Complete as for Jack Mittens beginning at **.

ABOUT THE DESIGNER
Peggy Bumgardner is mother to four fabulous sons and wife to a farmer. Playing with texture in her designs is her passion. Find her as Desertwindsong on Ravelry and at her blog: highdesertknitweardesigns.blogspot.com.

CLARA EARFLAP CHART

	RS: knit; WS: purl
▨	no stitch
╱	k2tog
╲	ssk
⋀	centered double dec: sl2 as if to k2tog, k1, pass 2 slipped sts over
○	yo
ⱴ	kfbf: knit into front, back, front of same st
V	RS: sl1 wyib; WS: sl1 wyif
ⱴ	RS: sl1 wyif; WS: sl1 wyib

JACK EARFLAP CHART

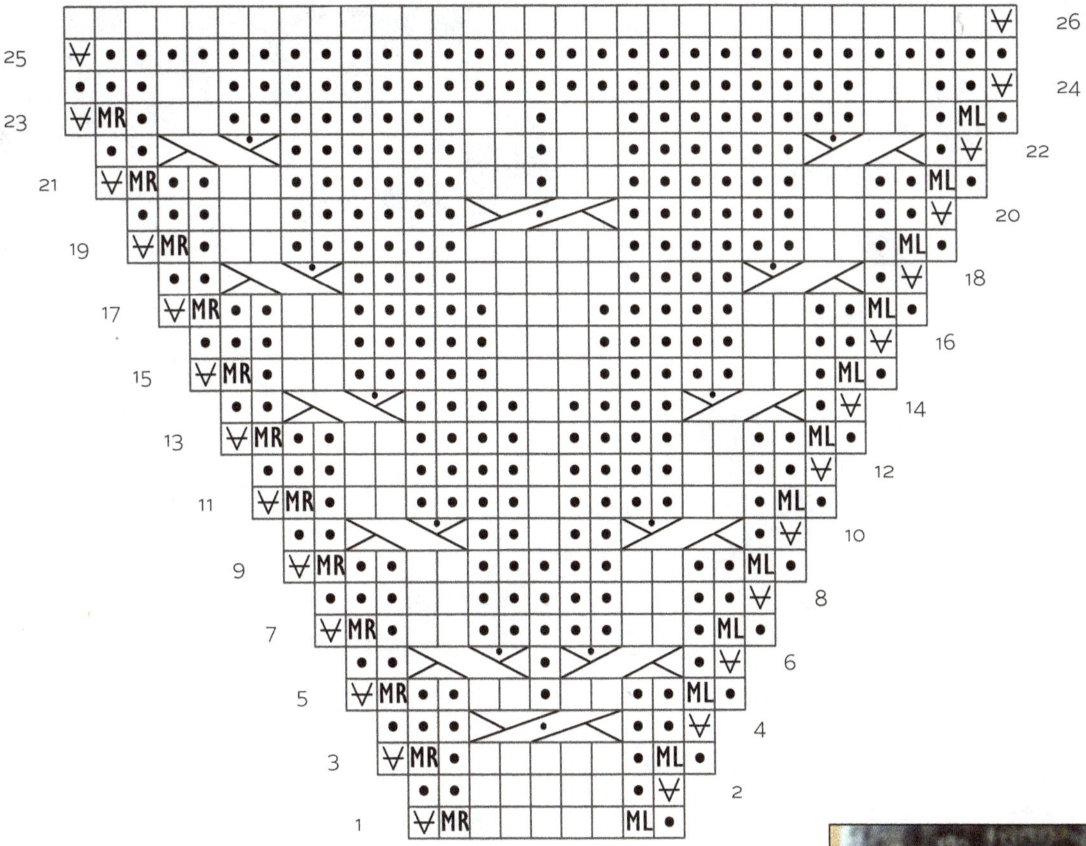

	RS: knit; WS: purl
•	RS: purl; WS: knit
MR	m1r
ML	m1l
⟩⟨	Cable 2 over 2 left p: sl2 to cn and hold in front, p2, k2 from cn
⟩⟨	Cable 2 over 2 right p: sl2 to cn and hold in back, k2, p2 from cn
⟩⟨	Cable 2 over 3 right: sl3 to cn and hold in back, k2, (p1, k2) from cn.
V	RS: sl1 wyib; WS: sl1 wyif
∀	RS: sl1 wyif; WS: sl1 wyib

SUSAN'S SUNSUIT
BY RACHEL HENRY

DIFFICULTY

INTERMEDIATE

Not long ago, my dear friend had her first baby. For Susan's first summer on the planet, I designed this lacy sunsuit, knit in lightweight yarn at a comfortably loose gauge. The bottom is knit flat, then joined and knit in the round following a simple diamond eyelet pattern. Diamond slip-stitch smocking cinches the top. Girly ruffles finish the edges, and i-cord straps are soft and adjustable.

SIZES
Approx age 3 [6, 12, 18, 24] mos. (shown in size 12 mos.)

FINISHED MEASUREMENTS
Chest 12.75 [13.5, 14.5, 15.25, 16]"/32 [34, 36, 38, 40]cm, unstretched (smocking pattern will stretch to fit)

MATERIALS
Three Irish Girls McClellan Fingering [60% merino wool, 30% bamboo, 10% nylon; 410yd/375 per 100g skein]; color: Isolde; 1 [1, 1, 2, 2] skein(s)

40-inch US #3/3.25mm circular needle
40-inch US #4/3.5mm circular needle

Waste yarn for provisional cast on
Cable needle (cn)
Yarn needle
Stitch markers

GAUGE
24 sts/32 rows = 4"/10cm in stockinette on larger needles
30 sts/48 rows = 4"/10cm in Smocking patt on larger needles, unstretched

STITCHES
I-cord:
Knit 1 row. *Do not turn work at end of row, but slide sts back to working end of needle, draw yarn tightly behind work, and knit row again.* Rep from * to * for desired length.

PATTERN NOTES
The sunsuit begins with a provisional cast on. The crotch is worked flat, then the provisional cast on is undone and the cast-on stitches picked up. The body is then knit in the round to the top edge. Pattern is written for the Magic Loop method on a long circular needle, but a short circular needle and dpns could be used if preferred.

Work all increases as m1 and all decreases as k2tog unless otherwise specified.

PATTERN
Crotch
Using your preferred provisional method and larger needle, CO 57 [60, 60, 63, 66] sts.
Row 1 (RS): Knit.
Row 2 (WS): Purl.
Row 3 (dec row): K1, ssk, knit to last 3 sts, k2tog, k1. 2 sts dec'd.
Row 4 (dec row): P1, p2tog, purl to last 3 sts, ssp, p1. 2 sts dec'd.
Rep Rows 3–4 another 10 [11, 11, 11, 12] times. 13 [12, 12, 15, 14] sts.
Work 1 RS row even.
Next row (inc row): P1, m1, purl to last 2 sts, m1, p1. 2 sts inc'd.
Next row (inc row): K1, m1, knit to last 2 sts, m1, k1. 2 sts inc'd.
Rep the last 2 rows 10 [11, 11, 11, 12] more times. 57 [60, 60, 63, 66] sts.
Stitches currently on the needle are the front of the sunsuit.

Lower Body
Undo provisional CO and place the resulting 57 [60, 60, 63, 66] live sts on needle with RS facing, for back of sunsuit. Knit across back sts, pm for beg of rnd, k57 [60, 60, 63, 66] front sts, pm for side, knit to end. 114 [120, 120, 126, 132] sts.

Purl 1 rnd.
Next rnd: *K2tog, yo; rep from * to end.
Purl 1 rnd.
Knit 1 rnd.

Upper Body
Work Rnds 1–12 of Smocking chart 3 [3, 3, 4, 4] times.

Sizes – [6, 12, –, 24] mos. only:
Work Rnds 1–6 of Smocking chart again.

All sizes:
Change to smaller needles and work top ruffle as foll:
Rnd 1: Knit.
Rnds 2–7: *K1 tbl, p1, k 1tbl; rep from * to end.
Rnd 8: *Kfb; rep from * to end. 192 [204, 216, 228, 240] sts.
Rnd 9: Knit.
BO all sts kwise.

Leg Ruffles
Using smaller needle, with RS facing, pick up and knit 1 st in every row around leg opening. Count sts and adjust to a multiple of 3.
Rnds 1–4: *K1 tbl, p1, k1 tbl; rep from * to end.
Rnd 5: *Kfb; rep from * to end.
Rnd 6: Knit.
BO all sts kwise.

Straps (make 2)
With larger needle, CO 5 sts. Work i-cord for 14 [14.5, 15, 15.5, 16]"/35.5 [37, 38, 39.5, 40.5]cm. BO.

Connector
With larger needle, CO 3 sts. Work i-cord for 3.5"/9cm. BO.

FINISHING
Attach straps to front of top. Attach connector to center back in an "M" shape (two loops—refer to photo above for placement). Weave in ends. Wash and block lightly. Dress baby, and kiss her.

ABOUT THE DESIGNER
Rachel (aka remcat on Ravelry) has been knitting for many years and enjoys trying new techniques. She splits her waking hours between her three young boys, her dogs, and her knitting. Her favorite place to knit in public is dog agility trials. Rachel is very grateful to her test knitters—Megan of DesignMegara, JennBelcher, and Ksana—for their help and beautiful test knits.

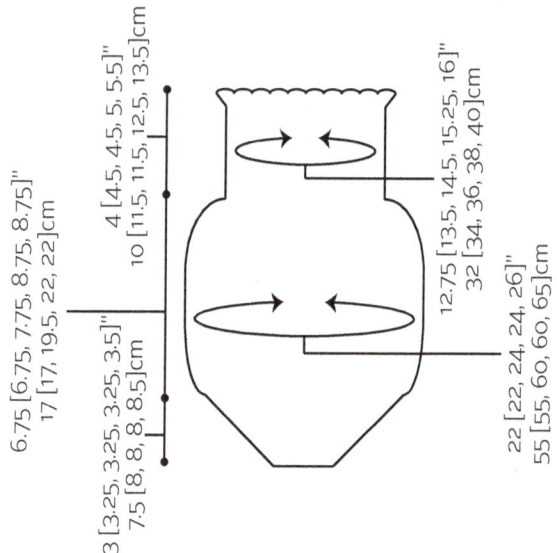

Next rnd: Knit across front, increasing 3 [0, 6, 3, 6] sts evenly spaced; then knit across back, increasing 15 [12, 18, 15, 18] sts evenly spaced. 132 [132, 144, 144, 156] sts.
Work Rnds 1–16 of Lace chart 3 [3, 3, 4, 4] times.

Size 12 mos. only:
Work Rnds 1–8 of Lace chart again.

All sizes:
Next rnd: Knit across front decreasing 12 [9, 12, 9, 12] sts evenly spaced, then knit across back decreasing 24 [21, 24, 21, 24] sts evenly spaced. 96 [102, 108, 114, 120] sts.

LACE CHART

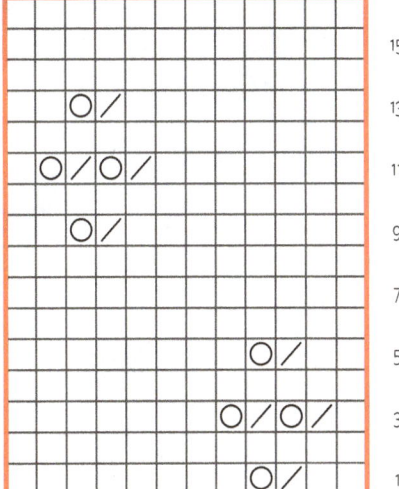

SMOCKING CHART

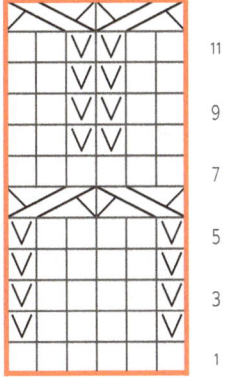

☐ knit

V sl1 pwise wyib

O yo

／ k2tog

⟩⟨ sl1 to cn, hold to front; k2, k1 from cn

⟩⟨ sl2 to cn, hold to back; k1, k2 from cn

☐ pattern repeat

BIRDBOOTS
BY SHARON FULLER

DIFFICULTY

INTERMEDIATE

These duck foot baby booties feature clever construction and (relative) realism. Birdboot is worked mostly in the round, with no seaming. The duck toes are simple cables (no cable needle needed!) with an i-cord for the hind toe.

SIZE
3–6 mos.

FINISHED MEASUREMENTS
Ankle circumference 4.25"/10.5cm
Foot length 4"/10cm

MATERIALS
Rowan Cotton Glace [100% mercerized cotton; 125yd/115m per 50g skein]; color: 832 Persimmon; 1 skein

32-inch US #3/3.25mm circular needle
Two US #3/3.25mm double-point needles for i-cord (optional)

Yarn needle
Stitch holder

GAUGE
25 sts/36 rows = 4"/10cm in reverse stockinette

STITCHES
Right Twist (RT):
K2tog, leaving both sts on left needle. Insert right needle between these two sts and knit first st again. Slip both sts off left needle.

I-cord:
Knit 1 row. *At end of row, do not turn work. Slide sts back to working end of dpn, draw yarn tightly across back of work, and knit row again.* Rep from * to *.

Judy's Magic Cast On
Full instructions with photos can be found at persistentillusion.com/blogblog/techniques/magic-cast-on/magic-cast-on-2

PATTERN NOTES
Foot is worked from the toe to the heel, beginning with a double-sided cast on. After foot is complete, stitches for the cuff are picked up around the ankle opening.

Pattern is written for the Magic Loop method on one long circular needle, but could be worked using dpns if preferred.

PATTERN
Toe and Foot
Using Judy's Magic Cast On, CO 44 sts (22 sts on each needle tip). Start the work with the purl bumps on the RS.
Set-up rnd: Instep (needle 1): knit all sts through the back loop. Sole (needle 2): knit all sts.
Rnd 1: P1, [k2, p7] twice, k2, p1; p1, p2tog, purl to last 3 sts, p2tog, p1. 2 sts dec'd on sole.
Rnds 2–3: P1, [k2, p7] twice, k2, p1; purl to end.
Rnd 4: P1, [RT, p7] twice, RT, p1; purl to end.
Rnds 5–7: P1, [k2, p7] twice, k2, p1; purl to end.
Rnd 8: Rep Rnd 4.
Rep Rnds 1–8 once more, then Rnds 1–4 only once, then Rnds 1–2 only once. 22 sts on instep, 14 sts on sole.

Heel and Ankle:
Next row: P1, k2, p7. Place next 2 sts (center of instep) on a holder and turn work. This is the new beg of row. Working back and forth on the 34 rem sts, decrease for ankle, then heel as foll:
Row 1 (WS): K1, k2tog, k4, p2, k16, p2, k4, k2tog, k1. 32 sts.
Row 2 (RS): P6, RT, p16, RT, p6.

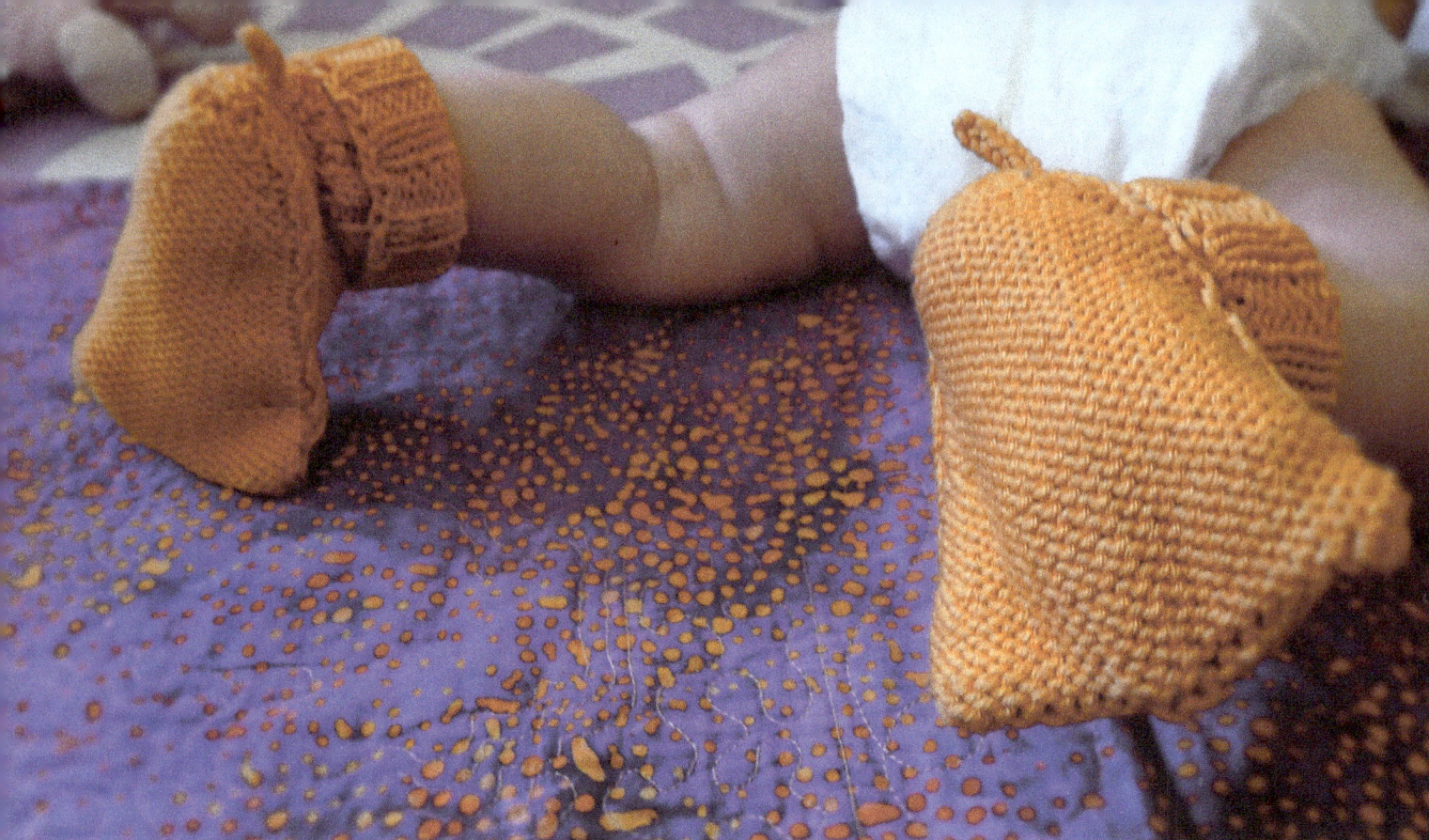

Row 3: K1, k2tog, k3, p2, k16, p2, k3, k2tog, k1. 30 sts.
Row 4: P5, k2, p16, k2, p5.
Row 5: K1, k2tog, k2, p2, k16, p2, k2, k2tog, k1. 28 sts.
Row 6: P4, RT, p2, p2tog, p8, p2tog, p2, RT, p4. 26 sts.
Row 7: K4, p2, k14, p2, k4.
Row 8: P4, k2, p2, p2tog, p6, p2tog, p2, k2, p4. 24 sts.
Row 9: K4, p2, k12, p2, k4.
Row 10: P4, RT, p2, p2tog, p4, p2tog, p2, RT, p4. 22 sts.
Row 11: K4, p2, k10, p2, k4.
Row 12: P4, k2, p2, p2tog, p2, p2tog, p2, k2, p4. 20 sts.

Work around the back of the ankle on first 7 sts only, picking up and decreasing out the center 6 sts, as follows:
Row 1 (WS): K4, p2, sl2 tog as if to knit, k1, pass 2 slipped sts over knit st, turn leaving rem sts unworked. 2 sts dec'd.
Row 2 (RS): P1, RT, p4.
Row 3: Rep Row 1.
Row 4: P1, k2, p4.
Row 5: Rep Row 1.
Row 6: Rep Row 2.

Graft the 7 working sts to the 7 sts remaining on the other end of the row. To graft in pattern, cut the yarn about 3 times the width of the knitting, plus about 8"/20cm. Thread yarn through a yarn needle. Hold the two pieces to be grafted in the left hand with wrong sides together and needle tips pointing toward yarn end on the right.

1a. Go through first st on front needle as if to knit. Leave st on needle.
1b. Go through first st on back needle as if to purl. Leave st on needle.
2a. Go through first st on front needle as if to purl, and drop st off needle. Go through next st on needle as if to knit.
2b. Go through first st on back needle as if to knit, and drop st off needle. Go through next st on needle as if to purl.

Rep steps 2a and b once more. 5 sts rem on each needle.
3a. Front: purl off, purl on
3b. Back: knit off, knit on
4a. Front: knit off, purl on
4b. Back: purl off, knit on
5a. Front: knit off, knit on

5b. Back: purl off, purl on
6a. Front: purl off, knit on
6b. Back: knit off, purl on
7a. Front: purl off
7b. Back: knit off

Note that the graft will appear to be a half stitch off kilter. This is because the stitches on the two pieces point in two different directions.

Cuff

Beg at center back of heel, with RS facing, pick up and knit 17 sts along one side of ankle, knit the 2 instep sts from holder, pick up and knit 17 sts along other side of ankle. 36 sts.
Next rnd: P1, k2, *p2, k2; rep from * to last st, p1.
Rep last rnd until cuff measures 2.5"/6.5cm, or desired length.
BO in pattern using the Russian method as foll (or use your preferred stretchy bind off): P2tog, return st to left needle, *(k2tog, return st to left needle) twice, (p2tog, return st to left needle) twice; rep from * to last 3 sts, (k2tog, return st to left needle) twice, purl last st tog with st in row below first st of rnd.

FINISHING

Hind toe:
CO 3 sts and work i-cord for 1"/2.5cm. Break yarn, leaving an 8"/20cm tail. Using yarn needle, run yarn through last rnd of sts and down through the center of the i-cord to the other end. Use tail to sew i-cord to center back of heel just above the cable.

Weave in ends. Block if desired.

ABOUT THE DESIGNER

Sharon Fuller works as a database developer and enjoys designing knitting patterns as another sort of programming. She brings a dressmaker's eye for detail and a love of surface decoration to her designs. Visit blog.sharonmattnadia.com or sharonf on Ravelry to see more of her designs.

FUNKYDS VEST

BY STÉPHANIE VOYER

DIFFICULTY
■■■□
INTERMEDIATE

Energy and colors. Kids are full of it and that's the inspiration behind Funkyds. Easy and fast to knit, a vest is a must in any kid's wardrobe.

SIZES
2 [4, 6, 8, 10, 12, 14] (shown in size 6)

FINISHED MEASUREMENTS
Chest 23 [25.5, 27.5, 29, 32, 33.5, 34.5]"/58 [64, 68, 73, 80, 83, 86]cm

MATERIALS
Babylonglegs Merino Aran [100% wool; 166yd/152m per 100g skein]; color: Vincent; 3 [3, 3, 4, 4, 5, 5] skeins

24-inch US #8/5mm circular needle
24-inch US #6/4mm circular needle
Set of US #6/4mm dpns

Cable needle (cn)
Yarn needle
Stitch markers
Stitch holders
Five ¾"/19mm buttons
One ½"/12mm button

GAUGE
19 sts/28 rows = 4"/10cm in stockinette with larger needles

PATTERN NOTES
Body is knit in one piece to the armholes, then back and fronts are worked separately to the shoulders.

STITCHES
RT-p (right twist purl): Sl1 to cn and hold in back, k1, p1 from cn.
LT-p (left twist purl): Sl1 to cn and hold in front, p1, k1 from cn.

PATTERN
Body
With circular needle, CO 143 [155, 167, 175, 195, 205, 213] sts.
Row 1 (RS): K5, *p1, k1; rep from * to end.
Row 2 (WS): *P1, k1; rep from * to last 5 sts, p1, k4.
Rows 3–4: Rep Rows 1–2.
Change to larger needles.
Row 5: K48 [51, 55, 57, 64, 67, 70], pm, k55 [61, 65, 69, 76, 79, 82], pm, knit to end.
Row 6: Purl to last 4 sts, k4.
Continue in stockinette with 4 sts at right edge in garter st until body measures 7 [7.25, 7.75, 9, 9.5, 10, 10.25]"/18 [18.5, 19.5, 23, 24, 25.5, 26]cm from CO, ending with a WS row.

Begin neck shaping:
Row 1 (RS): BO 8 [8, 8, 8, 9, 8, 9] sts, knit to end. 135 [147, 159, 167, 186, 197, 204] sts.

Sizes 2 [4, 6, 8] only:
Row 2 (WS): Purl.
Row 3: K2, ssk, knit to last 4 sts, k2tog, k2. 2 sts dec'd.
Row 4: Purl.
Rep Rows 3–4 twice more. 129 [141, 153, 161] sts.

Sizes – [–, –, –, 10, 12, 14] only:
Row 2 (WS): Purl.
Row 3: K2, ssk, knit to last 4 sts, k2tog, k2. 2 sts dec'd.
Row 4: P2, p2tog, purl to last 4 sts, ssp, p2. 2 sts dec'd.
Rep Rows 3–4 twice more. – [–, –, –, 174, 185, 192] sts.

All sizes:
Divide for armholes:
Next row (RS): K2, ssk, *knit to 2 [2, 2, 3, 3, 3, 3] sts before marker, BO 4 [4, 4, 6, 6, 6, 6] sts removing marker; rep from * once more, knit to last 4 sts, k2tog, k2. 34 [37, 41, 42, 45, 49,

51] sts rem for right front, 51 [57, 61, 63, 70, 73, 76] sts for back, and 34 [37, 41, 42, 45, 49, 51] sts for left front. Place right front and back sts on holders.

Upper Left Front
Row 1 (WS): Purl.
Row 2 (RS): BO 2 sts, knit to last 4 sts, k2tog, k2. 31 [34, 38, 39, 42, 46, 48] sts.
Row 3: Purl.
Row 4: BO 1 [1, 1, 1, 1, 2, 2] sts, knit to last 4 sts, k2tog, k2. 29 [32, 36, 37, 40, 43, 45] sts.
Row 5: Purl.
Row 6: BO 1 st, knit to last 4 sts, k2tog, k2. 27 [30, 34, 35, 38, 41, 43] sts.
Row 7: Purl.
Row 8: Knit to last 4 sts, k2tog, k2. 1 st dec'd.
Rep Rows 7–8 another 14 [15, 17, 18, 19, 22, 22] times. 12 [14, 16, 16, 18, 18, 20] sts rem.
Work even until left front measures 5.5 [6, 6.5, 6.75, 7.5, 7.75, 8]"/14 [15, 16.5, 17, 19, 19.5, 20.5]cm from first armhole BO, ending with a RS row.

Shape shoulder:
Row 1 (WS): P8 [9, 10, 10, 12, 12, 13], turn.
Row 2: Sl1, knit to end.
Row 3: P4 [5, 5, 5, 6, 6, 7], turn.
Row 4: Sl1, knit to end.
Place sts on a holder.

Upper Right Front
Replace held right front sts on needle and join yarn with WS facing.
Row 1 (WS): BO 2 sts, purl to end. 32 [35, 39, 40, 43, 47, 49] sts.
Row 2 (RS): K2, ssk, knit to end. 1 st dec'd.
Row 3: BO 1 [1, 1, 1, 1, 2, 2] sts, purl to end. 30 [33, 37, 38, 41, 44, 46] sts.
Row 4: Rep Row 2.
Row 5: BO 1 st, purl to end. 28 [31, 35, 36, 39, 42, 44] sts.
Row 6: Rep Row 2.
Row 7: Purl.
Row 8: K2, ssk, knit to end. 1 st dec'd.
Rep Rows 7–8 another 14 [15, 17, 18, 19, 22, 22] times. 12 [14, 16, 16, 18, 18, 20] sts rem.
Work even until right front measures 5.5 [6, 6.5, 6.75, 7.5, 7.75, 8]"/14 [15, 16.5, 17, 19, 19.5, 20.5]cm from first armhole BO, ending with a WS row.

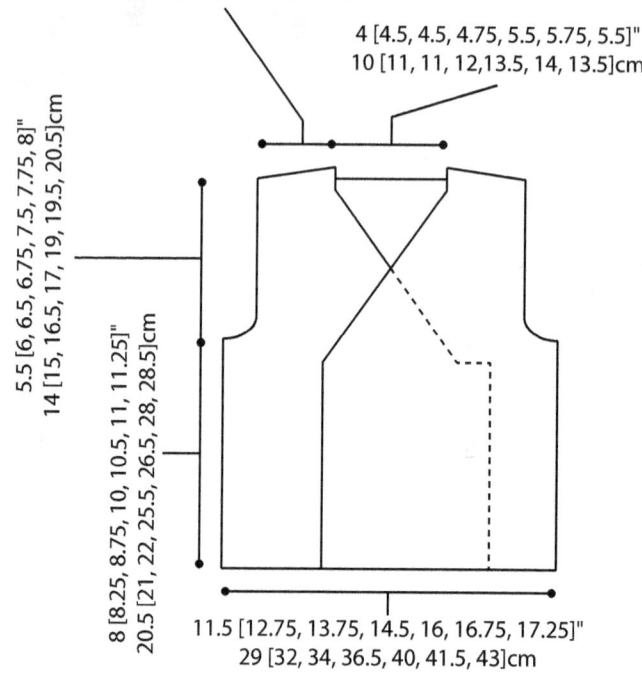

2.5 [3, 3.25, 3.25, 3.75, 3.75, 4.25]"
6.5 [7.5, 8.5, 8.5, 9.5, 9.5, 10.5]cm

4 [4.5, 4.5, 4.75, 5.5, 5.75, 5.5]"
10 [11, 11, 12, 13.5, 14, 13.5]cm

5.5 [6, 6.5, 6.75, 7.5, 7.75, 8]"
14 [15, 16.5, 17, 19, 19.5, 20.5]cm

8 [8.25, 8.75, 10, 10.5, 11, 11.25]"
20.5 [21, 22, 25.5, 26.5, 28, 28.5]cm

11.5 [12.75, 13.75, 14.5, 16, 16.75, 17.25]"
29 [32, 34, 36.5, 40, 41.5, 43]cm

Shape shoulder:
Row 1 (RS): K8 [9, 10, 10, 12, 12, 13], turn.
Row 2: Sl1, purl to end.
Row 3: K4 [5, 5, 5, 6, 6, 7], turn.
Row 4: Sl1, purl to end.
Place sts on a holder.

Upper Back
Replace held back sts on needle and join yarn with RS facing.
Row 1 (RS): BO 2 sts, knit to end.
Row 2 (WS): BO 2 sts, knit to end. 47 [53, 57, 59, 66, 69, 72] sts.
Row 3: BO 1 [1, 1, 1, 1, 2, 2] sts, knit to end.
Row 4: BO 1 [1, 1, 1, 1, 2, 2] sts, purl to end. 45 [51, 55, 57, 64, 65, 68] sts.
Row 5: BO 1 st, knit to end.
Row 6: BO 1 st, knit to end. 43 [49, 53, 55, 62, 63, 66] sts.
Work even until back measures 5.5 [6, 6.5, 6.75, 7.5, 7.75, 8]"/14 [15, 16.5, 17, 19, 19.5, 20.5]cm from first armhole BO, ending with a WS row.

Shape neck:
Next row (RS): K14 [16, 18, 18, 20, 20, 22], BO 15 [17, 17, 19, 22, 23, 22], knit to end. 14 [16, 18, 18, 20, 20, 22] sts rem each side. Place right shoulder sts on holder.

Left shoulder:
Row 1 (WS): Purl.
Row 2: BO 2 sts, knit until there are 8 [9, 10, 10, 12, 12, 13] sts on right needle, turn.
Row 3: Sl1, purl to end.
Row 4: K4 [5, 5, 5, 6, 6, 7], turn.
Row 5: Sl1, purl to end.
Place these 12 [14, 16, 16, 18, 18, 20] sts on a holder.

Right shoulder:
Replace held shoulder sts on needle and join yarn with WS facing.
Row 1 (WS): BO 2 sts, purl until there are 8 [9, 10, 10, 12, 12, 13] sts on right needle, turn.
Row 2: Sl1, knit to end.
Row 3: P4 [5, 5, 5, 6, 6, 7], turn.
Row 4: Sl1, knit to end.
Place sts on a holder.

FINISHING
Join shoulders using a 3-needle BO.

Armhole edging:
Beg at underarm with RS facing, using dpns, pick up and knit 1 st in each bound-off st and 3 sts for every 4 rows around armhole, ending with an even number of sts. Pm and join to work in the round.
Rnd 1: *K1, p1; rep from * to end.
Rep Rnd 1 twice more.
Loosely BO all sts kwise.

Neck edging:
Beg at right front edge with RS facing, using circular needle, pick up and knit 1 st in each bound-off st and 3 sts for every 4 rows up right front neck edge, across back neck, and down left front neck edge, ending with an even number of sts.
Row 1 (WS): *P1, k1; rep from * to last 4 sts, k4.
Row 2 (RS, buttonhole row): K1, yo, k2tog, k1, *p1, k1; rep from * to end.
Row 3: Rep Row 1.
Loosely BO all sts kwise.

Buttonhole band:
Beg at neck edge with RS facing, using circular needle, pick up and knit 49 [49, 49, 57, 57, 57, 57] sts along left front edge.
Row 1 (WS): *P1, k1; rep from * to last st, p1.
Row 2 (RS): *K1, p1; rep from * to last st, k1.
Rows 3–4: Rep Rows 1–2.
Row 5: Rep Row 1.

Sizes 2 [4, 6] only:
Row 6 (RS): K1, p1, k1, RT-p, p1, k1, p1, *LT-p, (k1, p1) twice, k1, RT-p, p1, k1, p1; rep from * 2 more times, LT-p, k1, p1, k1.
Row 7: P1, k1, LT-p, k1, *k1, p1, k2, RT-p, k1, p1, k1, LT-p, k1; rep from * twice more, k1, p1, k2, RT-p, k1, p1.
Row 8: K1, RT-p, p3, k1, p1, *p2, LT-p, k1, RT-p, p3, k1, p1; rep from * twice more, p2, LT-p, k1.
Row 9: P2, k4, *p1, k4, p3, k4; rep from * twice more, p1, k4, p2.
Row 10: K2tog, return st to left needle, use the knitted-on method to CO 13 sts, BO those 13 sts (this forms a button loop), *BO 9 sts, k3tog, return st to left needle, CO 13 sts, BO those 13 sts; rep from * twice more, BO 9 sts, k2tog, return st to left needle and CO 13 sts, BO those 13 sts.

Sizes – [–, –, 10, 12, 14, 16] only:
Row 6 (RS): K1, p1, k1, RT-p, (p1, k1) twice, p1, *LT-p, (k1, p1) twice, k1, RT-p, (p1, k1) twice, p1; rep from * twice more, LT-p, k1, p1, k1.
Row 7: P1, k1, LT-p, k1, *(k1, p1) twice, k2, RT-p, k1, p1, k1, LT-p, k1; rep from * twice more, (k1, p1) twice, k2, RT-p, k1, p1.
Row 8: K1, RT-p, p3, (k1, p1) twice, *p2, LT-p, k1, RT-p, p3, (k1, p1) twice; rep from * twice more, p2, LT-p, k1.
Row 9: P2, k4, *p1, k1, p1, k4, p3, k4; rep from * twice more, p1, k1, p1, k4, p2.
Row 10: K2tog, return st to left needle, use the knitted-on method to CO 13 sts, BO those 13 sts (this forms a button loop), *BO 11 sts, k3tog, return st to left needle, CO 13 sts, BO those 13 sts; rep from * twice more, BO 11 sts, k2tog, return st to left needle and CO 13 sts, BO those 13 sts.

All sizes:
Sew end of last button loop in place. Weave in ends. Block. Sew small button to inside of left front, corresponding with buttonhole on right front. Sew large buttons to right front, corresponding with button loops on left front.

ABOUT THE DESIGNER

Stéphanie Voyer is a knitter and designer from Montreal suburb. She has a fashion design diploma and by designing knits she has now find a good way to express her creativity and love of fashion. To see photos of her passions—her kids, cats and knitting—visit her French/English blog at www.alamaillesuivante.com. She is birana on Ravelry.

FIREMAN'S CARDI
BY TERRI KRUSE

DIFFICULTY
■ ■ ☐ ☐
EASY

When I started designing, I really wanted to come up with a cardigan based on the fireman's jackets that fascinated me so much as a child. This cardigan, with its contrast stripes, is just what I had in mind. It's a fun, yet wearable knit for the little ones in your life.

SIZES
Approx. 6 mos. [12 mos., 18 mos., 2 yrs., 4 yrs.] (shown in size 4 yrs.)

FINISHED MEASUREMENTS
Chest: 21.25 [22.25, 24, 25.25, 26.5]"/53 [55, 59.5, 63, 66.5]cm

MATERIALS
Squoosh Fiberarts Ultra DK [100% superwash merino; 225yds/206m per 100g skein]
- [MC] Burnished; 1 [2, 2, 2, 3] skeins
- [CC] Zest; 1 [1, 1, 1, 1] skein

24-inch US #6/4mm circular needle
Set of US #6/4mm double-point needles

Yarn needle
Stitch holders
5 [5, 5, 6, 6] 1"/25mm buttons

GAUGE
18 sts and 26 rows=4"/10cm in stockinette

PATTERN NOTES
This cardigan is a top-down raglan. Yoke and lower body are knit flat on a circular needle. Sleeves are worked in the round on dpns.

PATTERN
Yoke
Collar:
With MC and circular needle, CO 52 [56, 64, 68, 72] sts. Do not join.
Row 1 (WS): P3, *k2, p2; rep from * to last st, p1.
Row 2 (RS): K3, *p2, k2; rep from * to last st, k1.
Rep Rows 1–2 until work measures 1.25"/3cm, ending with a RS row.

Raglan shaping:
Set-up row (WS): P10 [10, 11, 12, 12] (right front), pm, p6 [8, 10, 11, 12] (right sleeve), pm, p20 [20, 22, 22, 24] (back), pm, p6 [8, 10, 11, 12] (left sleeve), pm, p10 [10, 11, 12, 12] (left front).
Inc row (RS): *Knit to marker, m1L, sl m, k1, m1R, knit to 1 st before next marker, m1L, k1, sl m, m1R; rep from * once more, knit to end. 8 sts inc'd.
Next row: Purl.
Rep the last 2 rows 12 [13, 14, 15, 16] more times. 156 [168, 184, 196, 208] sts: 23 [24, 26, 28, 29] each front, 32 [36, 40, 43, 46] each sleeve, and 46 [48, 52, 54, 58] sts in back section.

Divide body and sleeves (RS): Knit to first marker, remove marker, place 32 [36, 40, 43, 46] sleeve sts on a holder, remove marker, knit to next marker, remove marker, place 32 [36, 40, 43, 46] sleeve sts on a holder, remove marker, knit to end. 92 [96, 104, 110, 116] sts.

Lower Body
Purl 1 row. Change to CC. Work even in stockinette until body measures 1.5"/4cm from underarm.
Change to MC. Work even until body measures 3 [3, 3.5, 4.5, 5.5]"/7.5 [7.5, 9, 11.5, 14]cm from underarm.
Change to CC. Work even until body measures 4.5 [4.5, 5, 6, 7]"/11.5 [11.5, 13, 15.5, 18]cm from underarm, ending with a WS row.
Change to MC. Work 2 rows even.
Next row (RS): K3 [3, 3, 2, 3], *p2, k2; rep from * to last 1 [1, 1, 0, 1] sts, k1 [1, 1, 0, 1].
Next row (WS): P3 [3, 3, 2, 3], *k2, p2; rep from * to last 1 [1, 1, 0, 1] sts, p1 [1, 1, 0, 1].

Rep the last 2 rows until body measures 6.5 [6.5, 7, 8, 9]"/16.5 [16.5, 18, 20.5, 23]cm from underarm.
BO loosely in pattern.

Sleeves
Transfer 32 [36, 40, 43, 46] sleeve sts to dpns. Join MC, pick up and knit 2 [2, 2, 3, 2] sts from underarm, pm, and join to work in the round. 34 [38, 42, 46, 48] sts.
Knit 1 rnd.
Change to CC. Work even in stockinette until sleeve measures 1.5"/4cm from underarm.
Change to MC. Knit 1 [5, 0, 2, 3] rnds.
Dec rnd: K1, k2tog, knit to last 3 sts, ssk, k1. 2 sts dec'd.
Rep Dec Rnd on every 6th rnd 2 [2, 4, 4, 5] more times. 28 [32, 32, 36, 36] sts rem. AT THE SAME TIME, when sleeve measures 2.5 [3.25, 4, 4.75, 5.75]"/6.5 [8.5, 10, 12, 14.5]cm from underarm, change to CC.
When decreases are complete, work even in CC if necessary until sleeve measures 3.75 [4.5, 5.25, 6, 7]"/9.5 [11.5, 13.5, 15, 18]cm from underarm.
Change to MC. Knit 2 rnds.
Next rnd: *K2, p2; rep from * to end.
Rep last rnd until sleeve measures 5.75 [6.5, 7.25, 8, 9]"/14.5 [16.5, 18.5, 20, 23]cm from underarm.
BO loosely in pattern.

FINISHING
Button band
With RS facing, using MC and circular needle, pick up and knit 56 [56, 60, 68, 72] sts along right front edge.
Row 1 (WS): P3, *k2, p2; rep from * to last st, p1.
Row 2 (RS): K3, *p2, k2; rep from * to last st, k1.
Rep Rows 1–2 until band measures 1.25"/3cm.
BO in pattern.

Buttonhole band
With RS facing, using MC and circular needle, pick up and knit 56 [56, 60, 68, 72] sts along left front edge.
Row 1 (WS): P3, *k2, p2; rep from * to last st, p1.
Row 2 (RS): K3, *p2, k2; rep from * to last st, k1.
Rep Rows 1–2 until band measures 0.5"/1.25cm, ending with Row 2.
Buttonhole row (WS): Work 3 [3, 3, 3, 2] sts in pattern, *BO 2 sts, work in patt until you have 10 [10, 11, 10, 11] sts on right needle following BO; rep from * 3 [3, 3, 4, 4] more times, BO 2 sts, work in patt to end.
Next row: *Work in pattern to BO gap, use the backward loop method to CO 2 sts; rep from * 4 [4, 4, 5, 5] more times, work in pattern to end.
Continue in rib until band measures 1.25"/4cm.
BO in pattern.

Weave in ends. Block. Sew on buttons.

ABOUT THE DESIGNER
Terri spends her days knitting and designing. Her passion for knitting is met only by her passion for ice hockey. Find her online at throughthebackloops.wordpress.com and on Ravelry as ninja8tofu.

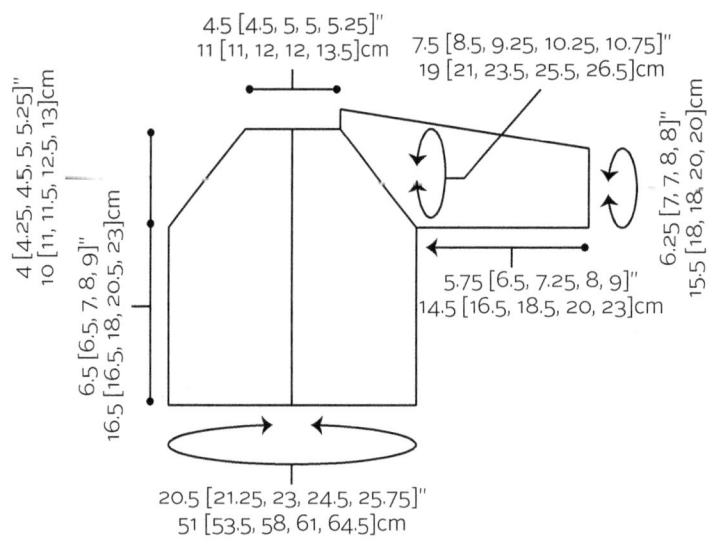

ACKNOWLEDGMENTS

Thank you to the designers who created such beautiful work for the book. Our biggest thanks to photographer Caro Sheridan and our charming models, not to mention their lovely parents. Abra Forman's considerable talents helped bring the project together in its early stages. Sarah Jo Burch helped keep things running so Abra and Shannon could get things done, and MJ Kim did a massive amount of organizational work before we handed everything off to the talented technical editor, Alexandra Virgiel. Elizabeth Green Musselman came late to the team but helped enormously with wrapping up loose ends.

The book wouldn't be nearly as beautiful without the yarns contributed by the companies below. Thanks to Make 1 Yarn Studio, in Calgary, AB, Canada, for providing yarn support for the Petal Bonnet.

We'd also like to thank the generous patrons whose Kickstarter support helped make this book series possible.

YARNS FEATURED IN THIS BOOK:

A Verb for Keeping Warm (http://www.averbforkeepingwarm.com)
Babylonglegs (http://babylonglegs.bigcartel.com)
Curious Creek Fibers (http://www.curiouscreek.com)
Louet (http://www.louet.com)
Pico Accuardi (http://www.picoaccuardi.com)
Rowan (http://www.knitrowan.com)
Stitch Jones (http://www.stitchjones.com)
Schoppel-Wolle (http://www.schoppel-wolle.de)
Schulana (http://www.schulana.ch)
Squoosh Fiberarts (http://www.squooshfiberarts.com)
Three Irish Girls (http://www.threeirishgirls.com)
Yarn Love (http://www.shopyarnlove.com)

ABBREVIATIONS

approx	approximately
beg	begin/beginning
BO	bind off
CC	contrasting color
cn	cable needle
CO	cast on
dec	decrease(s)/decreasing
dpn(s)	double-pointed needles
foll	follows/following
inc	increase(s)/increasing
k	knit
k2tog	knit 2 together
kfb	knit into front and back of the same stitch
kwise	knitwise
m	marker
m1	make 1 stitch
m1L	make 1 left
m1R	make 1 right
MC	main color
p	purl
patt	pattern
pm	place marker
p2tog	purl 2 together
psso	pass slipped st over
pwise	purlwise
rem	remain/remaining
rep(s)	repeat(s)
rnd(s)	round(s)
RS	right side
sl	slip
ssk	slip, slip, knit these 2 sts together
ssp	slip 1 knitwise, slip 1 knitwise, return both sts to left needle and purl together through the back loops
st(s)	stitch(es)
tbl	through the back loop
tog	together
WS	wrong side
wyib	with yarn in back
wyif	with yarn in front
yo	yarn over

ABOUT COOPERATIVE PRESS

partners in publishing

Cooperative Press (formerly anezka media) was founded in 2007 by Shannon Okey, a voracious reader as well as writer and editor, who had been doing freelance acquisitions work, introducing authors with projects she believed in to editors at various publishers.

Although working with traditional publishers can be very rewarding, there are some books that fly under their radar. They're too avant-garde, or the marketing department doesn't know how to sell them, or they don't think they'll sell 50,000 copies in a year.

5,000 or 50,000. Does the book matter to that 5,000? Then it should be published.

In 2009, Cooperative Press changed its named to reflect the relationships we have developed with authors working on books. We work together to put out the best quality books we can, and share in the proceeds accordingly.

Thank you for supporting independent publishers and authors.

We're on Ravelry as CooperativePress. Please join our low-volume mailing list and check out our other books at...

WWW.COOPERATIVEPRESS.COM

ABOUT FRESH DESIGNS

Shannon Okey wanted to do something to showcase emerging design talent after she left the editorship of a UK print knitting magazine; Fresh Designs is the result. A partnership between talented designers and primarily small/indie yarn companies (all of whom are thanked on the previous page — please help support these remarkable companies when you next shop for yarn), the first 10 Fresh Designs books have also broken the mold for designer compensation. Each time you purchase a Fresh Designs book or pattern, the designers receive a royalty share.

We hope you'll enjoy meeting the designers in these pages, and that you'll check out the other books in the Fresh Designs series.